FORGIVE or FORGET

Never Underestimate the Power of Forgiveness

FORGIVE or FORGET
MOTHER LOVE

WITH TONYA BOLDEN

HarperCollins*Publishers*

HarperCollins books may be purchased for educational, business, or sales promotional use. For information please write: Special Markets Department, HarperCollins Publishers, Inc., 10 East 53rd Street, New York, NY 10022.

FIRST EDITION

Designed by William Ruoto

Library of Congress Cataloging-in-Publication Data

Mother Love.
    Forgive or forget : never underestimate the power of forgiveness/ Mother Love with Tonya Bolden.—1st ed.
      p. cm.
    ISBN 0-06-019450-2
    1. Forgiveness. I. Bolden, Tonya. II. Title
BJ1476.M67 1999
179'.9—dc21   99-34892

99 00 01 02 03 ❖/RRD 10 9 8 7 6 5 4 3 2 1

To my friend, my love, my husband, Kennedy Rogers.
I am so happy we are able to forgive each other.

Lovingly,

Your wife

If you offend, ask for pardon; if offended, forgive.

—Ethiopian proverb

CONTENTS

Acknowledgments

I wish to acknowledge the following:
 God . . . who is at the head of my life and where all my blessings come from.

My fine, loving husband, Kennedy Rogers. Without him—well, when they said in marriage "the two shall become one flesh," that's us, and he feels good. I love you today, in the spirit of God always. Thank you for loving me.

My son, Jahmal, who makes me "keep it real" because to him and for him I'm Momma first (and Mother Love when he wants something). I love that you'll kiss me in public. I love you, Son.

My friend Alfred P. Lowman (I can use his entire name). Through our years of acquiring one another as friends, sharing, caring, agreeing to disagree, and laugh, laugh, laughing out loud, I know the love and respect we share with one another just gets better with time. Thank you, my friend—oh, and he's not too shabby a literary agent either.

Megan Newman, my editor at HarperCollins who (from my account) got the flow of Mother Love and truly believes like I do that each of us can make positive choices and changes in our lives and the lives of others—if we make an effort. Thank you for taking us on and allowing me to get the words, love, and wisdom out.

My new sisterfriend Tonya Bolden. When my friend Al Lowman said, "Mother Love, have I got a writer for you," he should have said, "THE" writer. She is real—real funny, real spirit-filled, real down and real smart. We are an excellent team—I, a brilliant storyteller, she a brilliant writer. I believe she is a true gem, blessed and brave. I hope this is just the start for us. (Yeah right. I'm doing good that she still calls me. Everybody wants her now—me and my big mouth.) I love you, Tonya Bolden—for being there, listening to me when what I had to say had nothing to do with the book, just being my friend.

Introduction

In early June 1998 I made my debut in the daytime talk show arena as the host of the successful nationally syndicated show *Forgive or Forget*. Definitely, it was a milestone in an amazing, skitter-scatter journey.

Me, a kid from the Cleveland projects who, along with three sisters and two brothers, was raised by a mother widowed at thirty.

Me, a young woman who had to leave college because she ran out of money—and then got pregnant.

Me, who realized she couldn't rely on welfare and whose work history included such plain-folks jobs as hospital housekeeper and school bus driver.

Me, who kicked into comedy on the heels of a dare, taking my gift for cut-up to a biker club on open mike night. And who would think that my on-the-fly routine at a bridal show would so knock out a radio station's program manager that he'd put me on the air? This is what happened in 1985 when I was shopping for my wedding gown (I was finally getting married to a good man: my favorite fella, my baby's father.)

So there I am at this bridal show at a hoity-toity Cleveland hotel, with a local radio station, WGCL, providing the entertainment. During a snag, the emcee got all tongue-tied, and started getting heckled (mainly by my mother). So I took the mike, putting Mr. Emcee, my mother, and about five thousand brides-to-be out of their misery with a sampling of my shtick and a little contest. Question: "Who's been engaged the longest?" I won that—thirteen years. Question: "Who knows her man the best?" That too I won—as I said to one young woman, "Eight months! You don't even know what his dirty laundry is like!"

Within two weeks WGCL's program manager had me answering "Dear Mother Love Letters" in the A.M., and reporting the weather and sports in the P.M. (When it was cold—"Put on your long underwear, folks." As for sports, I, never a sports widow, had a lot to say, like, "That bozo couldn't hit a baseball if it was as big as my head.")

After that, I went up and down the radio dial, from station to station. In between stations, I got booked to go on the road to do stand-up comedy. I was very funny, they said. Then, in 1989, I came off the road and into Los Angeles late-night talk radio.

I fell in love with Los Angeles right away (and it with me). My first subject was, "Why are there so many languages used on street signs in L.A.? This is America. Why not English?"—English is not our official language.

The press labeled me controversial. Mother Love, ha! Well, the controversy was on for the next fifteen months, Monday through Friday, 9 P.M. to 1 A.M., with me having my say and offering people advice on untangling their lives, flying right, and laughing out loud.

I took my no-nonsense, down-to-earth advice to print as well, with *Listen Up, Girlfriends!* and with my advice column for *The Globe*, a column that had a lot of folks listening up—more than ten million!

Along the way, I knew that this good journey was, yes, a result of talent and hard work but there was also an element of letting go—shedding a lot of luggage, releasing a lot of emotional hold-back. From childhood on up, I had suffered many calamities and had put myself through a fair amount of mistakes too. It was serious drama, issues that could easily have kept me bogged down and dreamless. The key to my escape from the blues and the blahs was—

My *decision* to forgive myself for the things I had done to myself—smoking, drinking, pigging out, drugs, crap.

My *decision* to beg pardon of folks I had wronged—wrongs committed when I was trying to do right and wrongs committed because I was stuck on stupid.

My *decision* to forgive those who had abused me, used me, stomped my soul, tried to keep me broke, busted, and disgusted.

When I was in the running to be the host of *Forgive or Forget*, I knew in my heart that this show was tailor-made for me. I had the nerve to believe that no one else could do it like I could because I just had this notion that this show would be a spiritual awakening and strengthening for me *and* you.

As the host of *Forgive or Forget*, I am part of a process that offers people a chance to resolve relationship problems, reunite with their families or friends, or at least come to terms with an issue and find the power to move on with their lives.

The people who come on *Forgive or Forget* come from all around this big mixed-up, spastic, glorious continent. They are married, single, divorced, and in-between. They are coming of age, middle-aged, and up in age. They are African, Asian, Caucasian, Hispanic, and in a panic.

People come to apologize publicly—to declare, *"I'm so sorry!"*—to a sister, a brother, a grandfather, a lover, an aunt, a spouse, a roommate. People come to demand an apology from Mama, Papa, Junior, Cousin Clyde, Daughter, and Godson Junebug. And these brave people know that the person they're apologizing to or demanding an apology from is backstage and usually listening to every word, along with a studio audience of 149 and a few million TV viewers.

As the guests tell us their stories, we ache for them, get mad at them, feel shame, even blame them. Then comes that moment of truth: when the one seeking for-giveness or asking for an apology ambles, tips, or slow dips over to that big wooden door. If, when the door swings open, the mistreated or the miscreant is behind it, then a new day has dawned. If the door opens only to air and that black drape, then the guest's request or apology was kicked to the curb. Either way, there are tears, fears, even jeers. Sometimes, there is laughter.

True, there's entertainment, but the show, I am proud to say, is not a buck-naked spectacle. Lives *are* transformed. Sure, I've seen fakers (but you won't see them on the show—we send them home on a bus). The real people, however—those who are serious about receiving forgiveness and those who are serious about forgiving—they leave the show with relief, and insight. When that happens, audience, staff, and crew—we've done our jobs.

This "we" includes our resident therapist. When you see that notice crawl up the screen during a break or before the credits—

A licensed counselor is made available to all guests of "Forgive or Forget" immediately following their appearance on the show.

—rest assured that it is legit. We would be remiss in our duties if we had people confront their anger, fear, and sorrow and then, when the cameras stopped, just gave them a soda and said, "See ya."

I am never privy to what goes on between the therapist and a guest. All I know is that I am comforted and relieved when men, women, and children who have bared their burdens talk with the therapist.

Sometimes I need a few minutes with the therapist, after an especially draining segment with a deeply wounded person: one of the legion who have come on the show, I believe, because they truly have no one to talk with, no one who loves them enough to listen to their grief, to serve as a mediator between them and that someone who hurt them. Guests have told me things on and off camera that they haven't told the producers. Guests have clung to my eyes and held onto my hug as if I am their lifeline. "I feel safe with you, Mother Love," so many have said.

Me? Yes, I get nervous. *Lord, don't let me mess up, let the words come to me*, I often pray. It's such an awesome, such a huge responsibility to guide lonely, hurt, disconnected people through their sorrows, to make them forget about the audience, forget about the cameras.

How do I hold up? Prayer, faith that God is holding my hand, and the knowledge that my mother-loving the people who come on *Forgive or Forget* can make the world a bit better.

It tickles and heartens me that when people spot me in the mall or the supermarket very often they ask for a hug before they ask for my autograph.

"Mother Love, let me tell you what my husband did to me."

"Oh, Mother Love, can you talk to my kids?"

"I need to come on your show, Mother Love—you not gonna believe my story."

After having done close to 200 shows (with 3 or 4 stories per show) I felt that it was time to write this book, get it all out at once instead of just in bits and pieces. This book is a chance to offer everybody who is interested some guidelines for embracing forgiveness, for latching onto its bounties.

In these pages, you'll meet some of the people who have appeared on *Forgive or Forget*. Along the way I also share with you some of my traumas, stumbling-blocks, renewals, and rejuvenations. And it is my hope that in the end, you'll be a true believer in the power of forgiveness—and that you'll *never* underestimate its power.

I love you!

Mother Love

PART I

Forgiveness: The Problem and The Power

Throughout the ages and from just about every place on the planet, we have received fine, pithy counsel on forgiveness.

Some anonymous soul said, "Forgiveness is the fragrance the violet sheds on the heel that crushed it."

Pennsylvania's founder, William Penn, eased in with, "Force may subdue, but love gains; and he that forgives first wins the laurel."

Another Quaker, Ben Franklin, clocked in with, "Men take more pains to mask than mend."

The very busy Friedrich von Schiller (dramatist, poet, historian) explained that "forgiveness is the finding again of a lost possession—hatred, an extended suicide."

Horace, that gentle poet of ancient Rome, cut to the chase with, "Anger is a brief madness."

Blessed Mohandas K. Gandhi warned, "If we practice an eye for an eye and a tooth for a tooth, soon the whole world will be blind and toothless."

Perhaps the best-known bit came from the eigh-
teenth century English poet Alexander Pope: "To err is
human; to forgive, divine"—the flip side of which the
fourth century Greek sage Saint John Chrysostom cap-
tured with "Mercy imitates God, and disappoints
Satan."

Some two thousand years ago Epictetus, another
Greek philosopher (and someone who had been a
slave), summed up the duty with these three words:
"Bear and forbear."

Sadly, many of us do not heed these wise words.
Forgiveness is not much of a priority for enough of us.

Lose weight. Pack on muscle. Beat back the aging
process. Get rich (the quicker the better). Own the
latest latest. This is the kind of stuff we tend to focus
on if we focus at all on self-improvement. But what
about the core? What about all the emotional and
mental muck that can make us flabby, old before our
time, spindly, and even poor? The anger and arrogance that hold us back from forgiving and seeking
forgiveness can really mess up our lives and make us
gruesome. In contrast, when we break free of anger
and arrogance, so much that is strengthening and
sustaining grows long roots—love, integrity, compassion, patience, wisdom. And let us not forget this:
peace of mind.

Making forgiveness (seeking it and giving it) a way of life is no cakewalk, because we live in a world where a whole lot of people regard meekness, tenderness, yielding, and looking out for number two, three, four, and forty-four as signs of weakness. Some of us even have the nerve to think that we are the stronger and the swifter for keeping a catalog of the injuries, injustices, insults, and slights we have suffered, as if it's a badge of honor to hold grudges.

What's more, when you spotlight the grudge-meisters' wrongdoings, they're prone to boast that their crap was justified, either because they were provoked or because it was par for the course in that fool's paradise "looking out for number one." Whichever way wrongs get explained away, back of it is the illusion that to apologize is to admit defeat, when in reality, to say "I'm sorry" is to be a decent human being.

Once upon a time, I thought that apologizing and forgiving came natural. I thought that when people did something wrong they naturally said, "I'm sorry" (and meant it). I thought that the person wronged naturally said they accepted the apology (and meant it). Then I grew up, and I found out how short we fall. I realized that apologizing and forgiving don't come natural and don't come easy.

With some more growing up, I also realized that these things are not *musts,* but *oughts.* You can exist without embracing the twin points of forgiveness, but you will not live if you do not. That's why I say forgiveness isn't a *must,* it's an *ought.* We *ought* to apologize when we harm someone, and we *ought* to forgive when we are wronged, and unless it is yearned-for behavior, learned behavior, practiced behavior, it will never become part of our core.

Very few of us come into an abundance of humility and mercy early and maintain it. This is understandable: we may be the height of Creation, but we are far from perfect. Plus, Planet Earth can be a very cold, cruel place. More forgiveness would surely make her a better place.

A friend once asked what I thought the world would be like if forgiveness abounded. I had to really let my imagination stretch on that one.

Just think . . . an everlasting spring, with lions lying down with lambs, with swords refashioned into ploughshares, and with Latrell Sprewell and Coach P. J. Carlissimo chatting it up over tea across the room from William Jefferson Clinton and his ace Kenneth Starr, who are playing Yahtzee and have plans to dine with David Duke and his good buddy Louis Farrakhan. Oh, what a world that would be. Indeed.

Do I think that we'll be there anytime soon? Nope. We can move toward it, though. Just imagine if, say, there were 20 percent more people saying, "I'm sorry," and 20 percent more people forgiving.

Would there not be more strong marriages? And wouldn't that increase the number of emotionally healthy children, which would boost the number of high-achieving, goal-oriented students, which would cause an uptick in the number of productive workers, intelligent managers, and dynamic entrepreneurs.

More forgiveness would give rise to more honest people because there would be more hope that if you confessed an error or an offense you wouldn't be savaged.

Fewer companies would knowingly send into the marketplace defective wares and tainted foodstuffs, because the more forgiving one is, the more compassionate one becomes, and compassionate people do not make money from items that no one would knowingly take for free.

We would also have fewer homeless people, because more people living fat and happy would be less unforgiving toward the needy, especially those needy who may have been the cause of their own downfall. Instead of wagging our fingers at a homeless drunk—"If you hadn't spent all those years boozing it up, you'd be liv-

ing in your own home instead of somebody's door-
way"—more of us would have mercy and devote our
time, talents, and C-notes to helping the distressed
recover and rediscover themselves.

Inasmuch as guilt and holding grudges are major
stressors, and what with some illnesses and ailments
being caused or exacerbated by stress, a lot of people
would see improvements in their health. The use of
legal and illegal mind/mood-altering substances would
decrease, don't you think?

Instead of bearing so much friction, this 20 percent
would be bearing more good fruit: they'd have more
time and energy for all kinds of creating—poems,
paintings, music, buildings, laughter, play, and sweet
love. Who knows what-all this Forgiveness Brigade
would come up with. Yes, just imagine a world in
which two out of every ten, or four out of every
twenty, or twenty out of every hundred, or twenty
thousand out of every hundred thousand people
made a habit of apologizing when they wronged
somebody and of forgiving when they were wronged.
There is just so much good power that flows from
asking forgiveness and offering it. And if we ever
needed more of this, we sure do need it now.

We are becoming increasingly intolerant. There are
the big *isms*—racism, sexism, ageism, homophobia—

which have folks wronging others and begrudging them their mere existence. This provokes the wronged and the begrudged to harbor rancor and sometimes to retaliate.

Also, there's a growing intolerance of little things. Madison Avenue has pumped us full of fool notions about achieving perfection, and this makes us more unforgiving of imperfections in ourselves and in others. And what you don't forgive, you come to despise. And what you come to despise, you're liable to harm.

Added to intolerance is the downside of our marvelous technological advances.

People don't need people as people once did. Technology now allows us to do more (and do it faster and better) all by our lonesomes. With our computers, faxes, TVs, VCRs, beepers, cell phones, and the Internet, we can retreat into our own little worlds and build our own little castles (with moats). The less contact we have with other people—the less we see their eyes and their tears, feel their breath (sweet or foul), hear their laugh or sigh, touch their bodies with a kiss, a pat, a hug—the less we relate, connect. The more distanced we are from one another, the less we matter to one another, and so the less compelled we are to forgive and ask for forgiveness, because individuals become more like abstractions. And who cares about relationships with abstractions?

Will you join the Forgiveness Brigade? Will you take up the challenge of making, not the whole world, but just your world a better place by choosing to make "I'm sorry" and "I forgive you" habitual?

Are you holding onto hurts?

Imagine letting them go, one after another, after another . . .

Let yourself feel free.

Are you weighed down by guilt over harm you've done to others and, as a consequence, ruined relationships?

Catch a vision of your misdeeds lifting up, up, and away, up and away . . .

Let yourself feel free.

Now, make a mental note of things you can do for others and for yourself with this new freedom. Hold onto this vision as you start the journey—a journey that begins with forgiving yourself.

When we forgive ourselves for the things we've done to ourselves and to others—family, friends, strangers, a stray dog—it's a lot easier for us to forgive others and seek the forgiveness of others.

Some people get eager to forgive others and apologize, yet they won't forgive themselves. For days, weeks, months, and years, they beat up on themselves for all kinds of things. As a result, they have all kinds of problems because they haven't addressed what's really going on in their heads. These problems may be physical. They may be emotional. They may be a combination of the two. Any way it comes, it's coming. There will be phantoms you cannot escape and weights around your ankles—stumbling blocks to apologizing and forgiving.

Generally, people who cannot forgive themselves half-step on forgiving others. They may say, "Apology accepted," but they remain in bondage to the Grudge Monster because they themselves have never known the liberty that forgiveness brings. Too, if you cannot forgive yourself and thereby experience the joy of true repentance, you cannot empathize with another's repentance. If you cannot forgive yourself, you're apt to project your hard-heartedness onto others and end up leery about seeking forgiveness. Do you see why I suggest that you start with yourself? And why I urge you to get inside yourself and clean out the crud?

I know women who truly regret having terminated a pregnancy (or two or three). Two, five, ten, twenty years may have passed, yet they still have not forgiven themselves. They are haunted. They suffer a sorrow that manifests itself in all sorts of ways, from overeating to making chronically stupid choices in mates.

I know former drug abusers who are still angry with themselves for the nightmare they put themselves through. Yes, they are clean and have gotten on the good foot, yet they can't fully enjoy their new self because they're still dogging themselves on the inside. Instead of having a more abundant life, instead of celebrating who they are and using the lessons they've learned in the service of others, they waste time dredging and drudging around in who they used to be.

I know men and women who years ago cheated once on their spouses and still they've not forgiven themselves and released the misdeed. Because they have not forgiven themselves, they deem themselves unforgivable, and there's the danger that they will put up with all kinds of nonsense from their mates if their mates are predisposed to being manipulative and vindictive.

Time and again on *Forgive or Forget* I meet mothers and fathers who seek the forgiveness of the children they have abandoned.

"Mother Love, I want to apologize to my daughter for leaving her when I was strung out on drugs."

"Well," says I, "what about forgiving yourself? Have you done that?"

"Oh, I can't even deal with that."

"Well," says I, "how are you going to be telling your child that you're sorry when you're not sorry, because you haven't faced what you did to yourself?"

(It's something else to watch them, to witness the light come on.)

"You know, Mother Love, I never even thought about me. It's not too selfish?"

"No," says I.

Definitely, it's not selfish to think about self, especially if your self is stuffed down, jacked up, whacked out. How can you help others get OK if you're not OK?

I had a friend who was molested by her uncle when she was twelve years old. She killed herself. She couldn't forgive herself for letting it happen, convinced as she was (with a lot of help from her mother!) that she had brought it on herself. I am convinced that if my friend had not blamed herself, if she had forgiven herself for thinking that she might possibly have done something that made that sick man think she wanted to be violated, she would not have tormented herself for three long years. She would not have ended up a fifteen-year-old suicide.

Far too often, the evening news carries the story of a husband and father who, finding himself unable to support his family, feeling at fault and a failure for being unemployed, shoots his wife and children and then turns the gun on himself. We've also had instances where a man or woman killed a former lover in the throes of the If-I-can't-have-you-nobody-can syndrome. The murder is fueled by rage: not merely rage at the former lover, but also rage at self, which is an indicator of unforgiveness of self.

Not everybody's failure to forgive themselves results in suicide or homicide. But all failure to forgive oneself results in some sort of distortion, fragmentation, or chipped psyche.

My whole everything changed when I learned to forgive myself and when I chose to make it a habit.

Over the years I have had to forgive myself for many things. My mountain was forgiving myself for disliking myself over my weight.

As some of you already know, when I was a kid I was stick skinny. I was so self-conscious. And other people didn't help any. Other people like this boy on whom I had a *big* crush. All I wanted him to do was pay me some attention and like me. He paid me some attention, all right: he would bag on me relentlessly. "If we put a hole in your head," he'd taunt, "we could put a thread through it and use you as a needle." He called me a chocolate Q-tip. He called me Olive Oyl.

I would just cry and make wild vows. "You just wait

until I get fat! One day I'ma be fat, and you ain't gonna be pickin' on me no mo'!"

My younger brother had sport with me too. Lots of times, while watching TV, I'd sit on the floor in something like a lotus position. My little (but big) brother thought it was the funniest thing in the world to run at me and bowl me over. He ended up doubled over with laughter as I, splayed out on the floor, burst into tears. He was around three; I was around six.

The fierce Cleveland wind had its way with me something awful, and this brought more shame. My sister was embarrassed to be on the street with me because the wind was always blowing me smack into a fence or upside a building. Sometimes it actually blew me up trees. Kids (and adults too) had a good laugh. To make matters worse, this being back when little girls rarely wore trousers, it meant I was getting an air job too. So there I was slammed against a fence or a tree, with boys grinning and snapping at my panties. At one point my mother sewed pockets inside my coat, to be filled with rocks on windy days. I wanted to gain weight *so* bad.

My mother wanted me to pick up pounds too; so she fed me and overfed me—

"You eat everything on your plate, young lady."

"But, Mama, I'm full."

"You're not leaving the table until your plate is *clean*!"

"But Mama . . ."

Like most poor folks' food, Mama's was full of fat, full of starch, even though we still ate lots of fruits and vegetables and drank plenty of water (OK, Kool-Aid).

I was coming up on fifteen when I started to gain weight, and as I did, my shape started coming in. (You couldn't tell me I wasn't hot stuff!) Then, as I neared eighteen, I got a little bigger, got more shape. (So much more to love!) When I hit twenty-five, the next thing I knew, I was a full-fledged fat person! And in this society that is *so* unforgiving about excess weight, I liked myself anyway.

All the women in my family are full-figured fine fat women. I remember my mother telling me, "Well, you've lost your svelte figure, now you really have to look good!" So I accepted the fact that I was never going to be a string bean again, and I understood that I was going to have to keep liking myself—my size, my girth—no matter what society might say. I decided not to let society tell me that because I was a size 18 I couldn't be beautiful, sensuous, and sexy. At the same time, I realized that I didn't have to become Gigantor, and self said to self, "Girl, if you're not comfortable with *all* the weight, go do something about it." I did. I began eating less, eating better. I remained a zaftig empress, but I became a healthier zaftig empress, and during this journey, I worked at forgiving myself.

First, I forgave myself for having been ashamed of myself as a child. Next, I forgave myself for years of overeating. And one day I'll forgive myself for not exercising (I'm still a work in progress too).

Then I moved on down the road to forgiving society for ostracizing me. I forgave the fashion industry for thinking that large women had no fashion sense, and only skinny one-bone women were attractive. (As I often heard Mama and her sisters say, "Nothing likes a bone but a dog, and he digs a hole and buries it.")

In and around all this, I forgave that little knuckle-head for tormenting me when I was skinny, my younger brother for bowling me over, my sister for being embarrassed to walk the streets with me on windy days, and Mama for overfeeding me with food that leads not only to fatness, but to diabetes, high blood pressure, and strokes.

After I became healthier and released the rancor, I became a better person in so many ways. Definitely my confidence picked up, and this empowered me. For one thing, I began talking with dressmakers and department store buyers about the need to offer stylish clothing for plus-size women. One thing led to another, and lo and behold I became a spokeswoman for a plus-size clothing line.

During my journey to a healthier Mother Love, I quit smoking, drinking, drugging—and I forgave myself for defiling my body. By now, a whole lot more of me was getting into shape: skin better, posture better, attitude better, better friends, better able to help other people better.

Hooking up with men who were not good to me and therefore no good for me was another thing I had to forgive my young self for. As I forgave myself for allowing myself to be dogged, self said to self, "You don't deserve a man who treats you any kind of way. You deserve a good man. You deserve a dedicated, loving, kind man. This is the type of man you should want." When I hugged up to this new attitude, a dedicated, loving, kind man was what I got. (And along the way, I forgave the men who had mistreated me.)

All this self-love had me on a roll. Soon I was off on tangents. I was getting into the habit of forgiving people for stuff that had nothing to do with skinniness, fatness, or bad romance.

I forgave the junior high school typing teacher who beat me up (badly) because I caught him humping one of my classmates.

I forgave my once favorite uncle for disappearing from my life.

I forgave a close close friend for stealing $200 from me.

I forgave another friend for lying to me about what happened to the $278.34 I gave her to pay my phone bill. She told me she'd gotten mugged (filed a police report and everything). But a few months later, I overheard her telling someone how she'd duped me big time. (The chick hadn't been mugged; she'd gone shopping with my phone money.)

In the mix, I started forgiving myself for things I had done to others. With this, I became increasingly comfortable (and eager!) to say "I'm sorry" and to make amends.

I apologized to my mother for having been a smart-mouth teen.

I apologized to the man who became my husband for the time I read him the riot act and said, "I don't need you!" (and other terrible things), and went on welfare to spite him, when he could full well take care of his son. (I was tripping.)

I apologized to a longtime friend for disrespecting her time and not keeping my word. This was during a business trip to my hometown. I had plans to go out to dinner with my friend and her new husband, but I let myself get careless (got a little full of myself). When I finished up my business, I left town—no dinner, no call, no nothing. It bothered me a lot, and then more when my sister told me how my friend and her husband had gotten all decked out and how excited (and then deeply disappointed) they had been when I didn't call. (I used to always call if I was running late or couldn't make it.) I felt like a heel, the bottom of a shoe. I called my friend and begged her forgiveness (and I sent flowers too), and she, ever gracious, accepted my apology.

None of this would ever have come to pass had I not cultivated the habit of forgiving myself.

Forgiving oneself isn't an overnight thing. The process varies from person to person, depending on one's mental and emotional fortitude. Me, I'm the kind of person who can take herself *all* the way down. I can lay myself raw open. I can be harder on myself than anybody else could ever be. Then, like the phoenix, I rise.

Me, personally, I talk to God.

"God, I know I did a horrible thing."

"God, how could I have done that to another person?"

"God, how could I have done that to myself?"

"God, am I evil? Am I horrible? Am I beyond redemption?"

"Have you abandoned me, God?

"God, do you not love me? Do I not love me?"

"God, show me the way, show me how to love."

I run it down. I cry. I jump up and down. I scream and holler. I have my fit. Then I get up, blow my nose, and fix my face. And I move on.

It's so cleansing to acknowledge your screwups. Also, the older I get, the less I need to take myself *all* the way down because another habit I've developed is learning from my mistakes.

Not everybody can go down deep, because some folks aren't able to bring themselves back up. They plunge into depression. They get caught in an unforgiving funk. Paused on ignorance. Stuck on stupid.

They can't rise because they become convinced that they don't deserve forgiveness. They come to believe that they have no right to forgive themselves. They conclude that they cannot expect others to forgive them and that there's no point in forgiving others because life is not a cabaret!

If you are of a delicate constitution, don't try to forgive yourself for everything all at once. Don't pressure yourself to start with the big issues, either. Take baby steps. Work your way up to bringing yourself down. Take it moment by moment, a day at a time. After all, we are works in progress.

As you grow in the practice of forgiving yourself, you'll find yourself doing a better job of asking others to forgive you. And if you have never really thought about the process (and potential pitfalls) of seeking forgiveness, then you do not want to skip the next section. If you do, you'll be sorry.

PART II

The Journey to Seeking Forgiveness

Pinch yourself and know how others feel.
—Japanese proverb

Do good and forget it; do ill and remember it.
—Maltese proverb

Forethought is easy, repentance is hard.
—Chinese proverb

If you are pure, if you are without spot or blemish, if you have never wronged anybody anywhere anytime, well, Mother Love beseeches you to say a prayer for us regular grunts out here trying to do this thing called life.

A lot of people mistake a short memory for a clear conscience.

—Doug Larson

If you are not a saint, no doubt you have done things or said stuff (probably both) that has caused another soul some pain. Your actions or utterances may have—

- *Caused someone mental and emotional anguish*

- *Cost someone a relationship*

- *Cost someone a positive opportunity*

- *Cost someone the loss of property*

- *Cost someone money*

- *Cost someone a job*

- *Caused someone physical injury and suffering*

If, because of you, any of the above has befallen others, then there's no two ways about it: you have done wrong.

A long habit of not thinking a thing wrong gives it a superficial appearance of being right.

—Thomas Paine

Wrong is not relative, I don't think. True, there are such things as extenuating circumstances. True, you may have meant no harm—even had good intentions. True, there are levels of wrong. Yet when you boil it all down, wrong is wrong. Am I right? (You know I am.)

But I'm preaching to the choir. If you had no sense of right and wrong, you wouldn't even be thumbing through my thoughts and observations. You'd have no conscience. You'd be a lost soul, one of those hopeless Homo sapiens who passes time on this planet without a clue, with only self on the brain. This is not you. The fact that you're reading this is evidence that you're interested in doing what you can to right some wrongs. You understand that seeking forgiveness is essential. I applaud you. I'm proud of you. And I believe that if you heed what follows, you'll see your way through and touch the freedom of forgiveness.

STEP 1

Recognize That Your Words or Actions Have Caused Harm

Where there is no shame, there is no honor.

—West African proverb

Even if your conscience is fried, when you've done something wrong you know it. You feel crummy, bad, slimy. Depending on what you did (and your temperament), whenever the misdeed whisks across your mind you may cringe, wince, or weep. As I said, whatever the offense, be it monumental or seemingly minuscule, you know it. Maybe it was—

• *Lying to your friend, sister, mother, father, boss, coworker, or classmate—or yourself—about something trivial or serious just to save your own sweet cheeks, or to make yourself look better, or merely to keep up appearances*

• *Stepping out on your girlfriend/boyfriend or your wife/husband*

• *Taking something from a loved one or a stranger that noway nohow belonged to you*

• *Backbiting and spreading dirt on a neighbor, a supervisor, a relative, or a casual acquaintance*

• *Breaking a promise*

• *Not repaying a loan*

• *Envying your neighbor, friend, or kin because, in your tiny unforgiving mind, she had just too many admirers, too much money, or was just too-too pretty*

• *Subjecting someone to physical, verbal, or emotional abuse*

- *Turning your back on Aunt Liza and Uncle John in their time of need—emotional, physical, or financial—when you could easily have assisted them*

- *Despising other human beings because of their race, ethnicity, religion, sexuality, political views, or socioeconomic status (the rich resenting the poor, the poor resenting the rich, the in-the-middle resenting both)*

I could give you a list two miles long because we human beings—we marvelous, mercurial, boneheaded, fascinating, puffed-up, ridiculous, fragile creatures—we can do stupid, belittling, outrageous, atrocious, fiendish, tacky things to each other—to folks we say we like, to folks we don't know, to folks we regard as enemies, and to folks we claim to love.

Every wherefore has a therefore.

—Yiddish proverb

You may not have committed any deeply despicable wrongs. If so, be glad. Don't get cocky, though.

Don't stop searching your memory bank. What about those "little" offenses such as the bit of gossip here, the half-lie there, the failure to give someone a message, the withholding of information, the betrayal of a confidence? These "little" things are wrong, and if you don't deal with them, they (just like the biggies) will deal with you. Maybe not now. Maybe not when you're ready, willing, and able, but oh, they will deal with you, and you will have to deal with them.

No doing without some ruing.

—Sigrid Undset

Yes, guilt. Guilt is a stubborn thing. Guilt can rock us, wear us down, bleed us of joy. Yet, guilt is not entirely a bad thing. Whereas the bad guilt induces mindless self-flagellation, the good guilt prods us to admit "I've messed up here." So the good guilt is a blessing because it lets us know that we are not lost causes and that we can become better people, if for no other reason than we realize we've caused a problem or we've been a problem.

> Truth, whether you perceive it or not, only brings light into your life.
>
> —Oprah Winfrey

Before you can reap the mercy, however, you have to face the misery. You will never shake guilt until you acknowledge that yes, you have caused harm. It's like anything else—from substance abuse and sex addiction to temper tantrums, midlife crisis, depression, and procrastination: recognition of the problem is the first step toward wellness. So look your wrongs in the eye. Name them. Say them out loud if you feel the urge. Be with it, face it, know it—then deal with it.

Transgression? Indiscretion? Faux pas? Abomination? Honest mistake? Stupid mistake? How would you classify the two, the twenty, the twenty-two hundred wrongs you've committed? Do this, and the guilt will begin to roll away.

Be brave and true about things. Don't downsize or minimize your wrongs, and don't rosy them up. Likewise, don't be overdramatic: don't make a prick a slash or a molehill a mountain; don't make your wrongs bigger than they are. Just honestly assess them before you confess them to others. And before you do that, it's critical that you forgive yourself. (If you're cloudy on this, swing back to Part I of this book.) As you do this, more of the guilt will roll away. Often it's only at this point that you recognize what the guilt was doing to you. And make no mistake, guilt will make itself manifest.

Take the young woman Leanette, who came on *Forgive or Forget* to apologize to her ex-boyfriend's mother, Ida, for violating her trust. Leanette had lied about what happened to the baby she was carrying, a baby her ex, and everybody else, especially her future mother-in-law, had been absolutely thrilled about. At first Leanette had been happy about her pregnancy. Then she started thinking that motherhood would seriously interfere with all her big plans, which included college and a career as a fashion designer. The prospect of having to scale back or abandon her plans altogether left Leanette less than pleased about being pregnant.

So one day girlfriend comes to her boyfriend and his mother with the sad news that she's had a miscarriage. Her boyfriend's mother is devastated by the news.

During the days and months to come, Leanette got sick all the time. Her skin broke out. She couldn't concentrate. She dropped out of college. Something was eating away at her. Something was killing her.

A clear conscience is more valuable than wealth.

—Filipino proverb

By the time Leanette came on the show, the burden she'd been bearing for a year was overwhelming—guilt. Guilt over having terminated her pregnancy. Guilt over lying about it, especially to Ida, with whom she had a bond that had endured even though she and the woman's son were history. I could see the guilt moving out more and more as she told her story. At one point I thought we were going to have to pick her up off the floor the way she cried and cried and cried: tears of repentance, tears of cleansing.

When time came to walk over to the door and find out if her ex's mother was willing to forgive her, Leanette slumped all the way to the door, head hung low. She kept her head down as the door opened.

The first thing girlfriend saw was Ida's feet. In the twinkling of an eye, Leanette was standing straight.

As the two women made their way to the sofa, Leanette's new attitude was so apparent.

There's not but 8 feet of floor between the door and the sofa. On average, it takes about 5.5 seconds. In those few steps, in those few seconds, Leanette was transformed. The guilt was gone.

A fault confessed is half redressed.

—Zulu proverb

Time and again I've seen people transformed right in front of me. I've seen them come out on the set with a load of guilt—weighed down, broken down, shut down—and as they apologized, I've seen them become lighter and brighter. It was that guilt coming up off of them. These people would never have reached this glory if they hadn't first acknowledged that they had harmed somebody.

Whatever you've done to others, call it for what it is. Lay it out raw. If you can do this all by your lonesome, well . . . get busy! If you need a hand, talk things through with a counselor, therapist, priest, rabbi, pastor, imam, friend, or relative. Maybe even

Mother Love. Just be sure it's someone trustworthy and wise.

If you think you couldn't possibly confess to the harm you've caused someone because it's just too horrible or, in retrospect, too horribly petty, think again. You are not alone. Nine times out of ten, others have shared the very thought—and lived to tell about it. I know this because I've lived a lot of life. I've seen, participated in, and been dragged into a lot of drama among my family and friends. Bigger than this are all the wrongs I've witnessed people fess up to and apologize for on *Forgive or Forget*. Here's a sampling:

- *Heather said, "I'm sorry" to her friend, Kelly, for bailing out of Kelly's wedding at the eleventh hour.*

Kelly was devastated when, on the morning of her wedding day, she got word that Heather, a friend since seventh grade, was too sick to keep her date as bridesmaid. Kelly was doubly crushed when she found out the real reason for Heather's no-show: Heather, very much in the pink, had preferred to go partying. All this happened four months before Heather came on *Forgive or Forget* seeking Kelly's forgiveness. For Kelly, this was too soon. "I can't forgive you, Heather," she said. "This is too open. . . . It hurts too much." Kelly's husband, Sam, was in the audience, and he agreed with his wife's decision 100 percent.

· *Andreanna asked her sister, Rhonda, to forgive her for doing the do with Rhonda's first love.*

As Andreanna frankly admitted, she didn't have a relationship with her sister's boyfriend, just sex (with one encounter resulting in a baby boy). Jealousy, years of raging jealousy, was the spark: Andreanna had been jealous of Rhonda because their mother raised Rhonda and not her. Also, Andreanna had always thought that Rhonda was prettier than she. After Rhonda forgave her sister, one audience member gave Andreanna a pat on the back and told her to count her blessings. "Not many people get the chance to be forgiven," the woman said. (And this is why I love hosting *Forgive or Forget*. I get to move that "not many" to more. I get to help increase of peace.)

· *Sam asked his ex-fiancée, Brandy, to forgive him for cheating on her—with her younger sister!*

Sam was at Brandy's house, waiting for her, when he and Brandy's little sister started talking about matters of the heart and intimacies. "Somehow, we ended up kissing," said the very sorry Sam. Then, "somehow," the two "found" themselves naked . . . then, in the bedroom . . . then, in the bed . . . then— caught in the act by Brandy, who'd been "saving" herself for Sam. "Tears just came flying out. The yelling began. And that's when I got outta there," said Sam, as he recounted what he referred to as "the biggest mistake of my life." Now, Sam wanted Brandy to forgive him and take him back. If a friendship was all Brandy could offer, Sam would be grateful for that, he said. At it turned out, friendship was what Brandy had to offer when she came through the door. While she could forgive him, she didn't feel that could trust him again in romance. "You can learn a lot from this,"said a man in the audience who was very sympathetic to Sam and Brandy, and they, who'd been holding hands all the while that they sat on the sofa, agreed.

- *Otis apologized to his ex-girlfriend, Cynthia, for sneaking around and checking up on her.*

Otis put himself and his girl through two years of unfounded jealousy. During this time he did such things as hide behind trees outside Cynthia's work place to watch her comings and goings and with-whomings. His feeble defense was that he'd been dogged by women in the past. The audience had absolutely N-O sympathy for I-Spy guy, and even applauded when Cynthia was not behind the door.

· *Clyde apologized to his father, Terry, for falsely accusing him of stealing his girlfriend.*

This story is a reminder that we should look and look again before we leap to conclusions. And how refreshing it was to see two big manly-men being so tender (hugging tightly, holding hands) as they put the past behind them.

· *Beth apologized to her mother, Linda, for falsely accusing her of child abuse.*

Beth's accusation resulted in Linda's being dragged from her home by the police, hauled off to jail, and ultimately losing of custody of Beth, then 16. Beth put her mother through this because she wanted her freedom. And the kicker is this: Linda didn't contest the charges because she thought doing so would get Beth in deep trouble. So Beth lived in a group home until she was 18 (having more freedom and, I suspect, finding out that freedom is overrated). By the time Beth came on the show, she had definitely grown up, having recently wrenched herself out of a relationship with an abusive man and trying her darnedest to be a good mother to her son. Yes, having a child of her own had given her new insights on motherhood. This, however, was only part of the reason Beth was so on fire to apologize to her mother and renew their relationship. You see, Beth had recently found out that her mother had been diagnosed with cancer. Beth was beyond joy when her mother forgave her fully.

- *Bruce apologized to his daughter and son, Karen and Scott, for choosing booze and partying over them for fourteen long years.*

Bruce, the son of an alcoholic and abusive man, had been abusing alcohol for thirty-odd years. And Bravo for Bruce! He turned from his vices before he asked for Karen and Scott's forgiveness. Bruce had been sober for fourteen months when he came to *Forgive or Forget.* Karen and Scott were behind the door, ready, eager to have a relationship with their dad. Their inspiration to forgive and to love was, they said, the commandments and teachings of Jesus.

• *Debbie begged her three children to forgive her for being an awful mom.*

Debbie went from depression to alcohol and drug abuse to being AWOL for days at a time—this when all her children were under the age of 13. The oldest child, Stacy, had to grow up fast. She mothered as best she could herself and her little brothers, T.J. and Ricky, and she eventually became their legal guardian. In the meantime, Debbie's efforts to straighten up were unsuccessful. A year before she came on *Forgive or Forget*, Debbie tried to reunite with her children. Changed locks and telephone number was their response. It was something else to see Stacy, T.J., and Ricky walk through the door. True, their trepidation and lingering anger were very much in evidence, particularly T.J.'s. He admitted that while he forgave his mother, he didn't yet believe that she would really get herself together and stay together and be the mom they needed.

• *Charisse apologized to her mother, Susan, for being an out-of-control teen.*

How many of us have wanted to or needed to do this. (It's not too late.)

> · *Natasha apologized to her mother, Rita, for refusing*
> *to change her wedding date so that her mother could*
> *attend.*

It wasn't as if Natasha's plans had been many months in the making. Natasha's fella proposed on a weekday (after two months of dating), and the two made fast plans for a wedding the coming weekend. The wedding day clashed with Rita's church commitments she couldn't break, and she asked her daughter (her oldest child and so the first to marry) to move the wedding back one week. One little week. "Back then, I was stubborn and selfish," Natasha confessed. She also admitted that she'd had a serious "attitude problem." Since then, she'd come into a good deal of maturity, very much helped along by the fact that she was now a mother herself. Rita, a gracious, long-suffering type woman forgave her daughter. (And when I encouraged Natasha to throw another wedding that her mother could help her plan—and attend!—Natasha let it be known that she was way ahead of me.)

> · *Theresa apologized to her half-siblings for being*
> *jealous of them when she was younger.*

I sometimes think the unseen, passive transgressions such as envy and covetousness are the most difficult for us to acknowledge to others as well as to ourselves.

> • *Enrique apologized to his wife, Juanita, for years of physical abuse during their twenty-one, going on twenty-two, years of marriage.*

Enrique and Juanita were 18 and 16 when they married, and Enrique, who'd grown up in a home where physical abuse was a normal means of communication, thought being the man of the house meant being violent. He hit his wife in the home, he hit her in front of their five children, he hit her in front of relatives, he hit her in front of strangers. In 1991 he stopped the violence and began to get help. Still, wounds were deep, and by the time Enrique appeared on *Forgive or Forget*, Juanita was on the verge of leaving him. For seven years he had been trying to heal and rebuild his family—a family that included a teenage son who was showing signs of following in his father's old footsteps and a daughter who was showing signs of a possibly fatal attraction to abusive men. Juanita was at the end of her rope, afraid to hope for joy. Enrique, who'd lost some forty pounds from the sweating and fretting, laid it out raw. He took complete responsibility for his actions; he pleaded with Juanita to remain his wife and hold his

hand as he continued his journey to wholen[...]
retiring Juanita was, to the surprise of ma[...]
the door. "I am *so* sorry for all the abuse I put you through," Enrique practically wept as he and Juanita sat on the sofa. "I want to grow old and die with you," he told her. Said Juanita to her husband, "I do love you or I wouldn't be here." This couple went through such a transformation. They became friends of the show as well, keeping us abreast of what's happening in their lives—how Enrique continues to live forgiveness.

- *Alicia apologized to her husband, Earl, for being physically abusive and controlling.*

The last time Alicia jumped Earl, instead of doing his usual shrug-off, he struck back—to her head. And his blow left Alicia (five months pregnant at the time) with Bell's palsy. This was truly a very sad case. Also sad was the fact that it took Earl leaving Alicia for her to come around and say, "I'm sorry," and to get into therapy. And it took this segment for a lot of folks to realize that men also get battered. Abuse is wrong, against anyone. By the way, Earl did not come through the door.

- *Cindy asked her sister Chris to forgive her for disappearing for several years.*

Cindy was four when, as she said, her mother "kicked her out of the house" (how a little child can be kicked out of the house is beyond me). Eventually, Cindy was placed in foster care, and when Chris was in a position to take Cindy in she did. Chris gave Cindy not only food shelter and clothing, but also a heap of mother-love. Cindy moved out on her own when she was 18 and after a while she began to show her sister no respect, badmouthing her to boot. Then, one day Cindy just up and—poof!—she was gone. For four years Chris didn't know if her little sister was dead, damned, or delivered. Cindy was profoundly sorry. She admitted that she'd spiraled into a pit of selfishness and spite, and that she'd been running away from love. (What a high note this segment ended on: sisters reunited and Chris beholding a treasure she didn't know she had—Cindy's one-year-old daughter, Destiny.)

- *Edward begged pardon of his brother Will for persecuting him (physically and verbally) because he was gay.*

One time Edward lost it to the point that he started beating his brother with a lamp! Edward was very uncomfortable with gayness, but at the heart of his rage was the fact that his brother never told him out-right that he was gay but sort of let it slip up on Edward. Edward's fury had left him estranged from his brother and other family members for years. Edward came on *Forgive or Forget* because he no longer wanted to live that way. He wanted to be a part of his family again, and he knew the only way that could possibly happen was for him to "start mending," as he put it. The first thing he had to repair was his relationship with his brother Will. "I want my brother back," Edward said. And Will forgave him.

- *Jaime begged her husband, Russell, to forgive her for being lazy and for being nasty to him.*

It wasn't until hubbie left her (and their children) that Jaime got busy repenting of her sorry ways, and it was too little, too late. When Jaime returned from the empty door, she cried something awful. I urged her to look ahead and to the welfare of her children. I rallied her to believe that she could heal in time, if she wanted to.

- *Debbie apologized to her daughter, Amanda, for forcing her to enter beauty pageants during her entire childhood.*

Debbie's daughter was still very angry about that and she refused to accept her mother's apology.

- *Sherry apologized to her sister Debra for introducing her to crack-cocaine.*

About ten years prior to their appearance on *Forgive or Forget*, Sherry, already well acquainted with crack-cocaine, introduced her sister to this drug. Both sisters dug deep into the habit, drugging it up daily for six years, during which time Debra made a mess of her once good, prosperous life with her husband and two sons. Debra got clean before Sherry did, and she got her life back together. Sherry hadn't been so successful. She'd been clean for a mere three months when she appeared on the show, looking a hundred hard years old. The sisters hadn't seen each other for about eight years, and when they left the show we had the feeling that they might never see each other again, for Debra did not mince words when, from backstage, she told her sister why she had not come through the door. "[There's] nothing that comes out of your mouth that I believe," said Debra. "You're evil and I'll never, ever trust you. I don't believe a word that you said on this program."

- *Linda apologized to her ex-boyfriend's sister, Joan, for robbing her house and stealing her van, which Linda and her ex proceeded to use in a cross-country crime spree.*

More than a decade had passed since Linda ripped off Joan, who had treated her "like a sister." At the time, Linda and Joan's brother were not only partners in crime but also partners in drugs. Both ended up serving time for their deeds. After Linda's two years in jail she was a changed woman and embarked on a legal life. In the meantime, Joan "hurt a lot of years." This is what Joan said after she came through the door with forgiveness for Linda. Joan also admitted that ten years go she wouldn't have been able to forgive Linda. When an audience member asked Linda why it had taken so long for her to give Joan a sincere apology, Linda replied, "fear." When another member of the audience asked Linda why she'd shown up empty-handed (after all, she had stolen thousands of dollars in cash and merchandise), Linda admitted that she hadn't thought about (and with all eyes trained on her, Linda said she'd get busy.)

- *Shelander apologized to her sister-in-law Gwendolyn for seven years of rudeness and emotional abuse.*

Shelander was one of the most penitent and honest people I've ever seen. She acknowledged that she'd been simply ornery (she was great friends with her brother's previous girlfriend). What made Shelander's guilt all the more heavy was that her sister-in-law had been nothing but an angel throughout, and true to form Gwendolyn forgave Shelander. How had Gwendolyn managed the ordeal? "I just prayed and waited for God to work things out," she said.

A very precious segment was when six-time Grammy winner Florence LaRue, of The 5th Dimension, apologized to her friend Mary Ann for not being there when Mary Ann most needed her. This little story had a powerful message, especially for those knuckleheads who think there's no point in apologizing for what someone doesn't even know was done to them. Listen up, all you who say, "Let sleeping dogs lie." Florence LaRue reminded us that sleeping dogs can bite.

Florence had been friends with Mary Ann since childhood. As a grown-up, Florence also became close friends with Mary Ann's husband, Burney. Florence said that the couple was her getaway, her "touch of reality." Mary Ann and Burney never tried to trade on their friendship with Florence and never schemed to show off their celebrity friend when Florence paid them a visit.

Understandably, when Burney died, Mary Ann expected Florence to attend his funeral. Florence didn't. She told Mary Ann that work would not permit—which wasn't exactly the whole truth and nothing but the truth. Her schedule had been tight, but it hadn't been *that* tight. And so she came on *Forgive or Forget* to tell Mary Ann the truth and ask her forgiveness. Being the class act she is, Florence came with a loving bouquet of long-stemmed red roses.

As I watched Mary Ann listening to Florence's confession, and as I listened to the kind of person Florence said Mary Ann had always been, I was pretty sure that Mary Ann was going to forgive Florence and keep on loving her.

Mary Ann was indeed behind the door. The two friends hugged, and Mary Ann loved smelling her roses.

What had Mary Ann felt about Florence's no-show to Burney's funeral? "At first I was a little upset," Mary Ann admitted, but then she let it go. When I asked Florence about the guilt, she said that it was compounded by the fact that Mary Ann had been so understanding, had never given her any grief whatsoever.

As this lovefest was going on, an audience member asked Florence why she hadn't just let sleeping dogs lie. What you don't know can't hurt you, right?

A half-truth is a whole lie.

—Yiddish proverb

"The closer I get to God," Florence explained, "the more He lets me see that honesty is truly the right thing." She went on to say that "all the fame, all the fortune in the world is not worth the honesty I have with this woman. She is my friend. I can't lie to her. I had to let her know that there was a slight possibility that I could have been there. I have to know in my heart that I have been honest with her." And Florence LaRue's guilt went up, up, and away.

STEP 2

Don't Make Excuses

Excuses are tools of incompetence that build monuments of nothing.ness

—Anonymous

Excuses, excuses, excuses.

One of the things that holds us back from fully acknowledging wrongdoing and making an apology is the allure of excuses. As you reconstruct what led up to the wrong you did, you may be tempted to start feeling sorry for yourself and making excuses. True, there may be reasons—and very understandable reasons—behind the wrong you committed; however, there is no excuse.

"Hold on, Mother Love, you didn't hear how she talked about me."

"Wait one quick minute, Mother Love, you didn't see me with my raccoon eyes and bloodied lip."

"Mother Love, cutting up the clothes of that #$#%$ ain't half as evil as what he did—bringing that @#@#!$ up in my house!"

Excuses are always mixed with lies.

—Arab proverb

"OK, Mother Love, maybe I shouldn't have smacked her, but Mother Love, she went out and charged up *eight hundred dollars* worth of clothes when we can't hardly make ends meet. That heifer is lucky I didn't stomp her behind."

"See, the thing is, Mother Love, I was on my last dime, and I knew my mother didn't need that twenty."

"Mother Love, I know I promised I wouldn't tell anybody about her problem, but I told only one person—and that was because I thought she could help."

"It was a joke, Mother Love. I was just getting them back for a prank they played on me."

He who makes excuses accuses himself.

—French proverb

I have heard so many and too many excuses. Admittedly, owning up to the wrong you've done isn't easy—especially when the person you have wronged has also wronged you. These situations call for a huge helping of Mother Love.

Your serving will include—courage, strength, *and* a reality check.

I believe you have it in you.

Granted that sorry Sarah may have put your business in the street and at the time you thought badmouthing her was the appropriate response. Yes, low-life Larry was wrong for cheating on you. (We all know he's pond scum.) And yes, I can see why you flipped when your sister told that *bald-faced* lie. But dig this: you were wrong to have committed a wrong in return. It's what we learned as children: two wrongs don't make a right. No matter what someone has done to you, retaliation, revenge, payback—whatever word you like—is W-R-O-N-G. Period. (Remember Martin Luther King, Jr.'s paraphrase of Gandhi's gem: "An eye for an eye leaves everybody blind.")

What if the wrong you committed was beyond your control? For instance, when you promised to buy your niece a computer, you had every intention of doing it, but then your car broke down, and you didn't get in as much overtime as you'd planned. Your niece doesn't understand all this grown-up mess. She knows Auntie is getting that computer and she's going to be surfing with the quickness. You know you've messed up—your credibility will be questioned, your word means little, and her cute face is cracked. What do you do now? Don't pretend you didn't make a promise and don't act like she misunderstood. Be honest. Be real. Tell her you messed up and that you will keep your word.

> To rush into explanations and excuses is always a sign of weakness.
>
> —Agatha Christie

Once you own up to the fact that you have harmed someone, once you refuse to make excuses, then you are ready to move forward with seeking the forgiveness of the person you've wronged.

STEP 3

Repentance Is More Than Regret

Plenty of people come up quick with an apology when they get busted. They come up with apologies and galloping promises (and excuses) because they want to avoid a confrontation. A child might want to avoid a spanking or the loss of privileges; an adult might want to avoid getting hit, fired, left, talked about, or tongue-lashed. In truth, the only thing you're sorry about is that you got caught.

If you're scrambling to be forgiven before you've processed the matter, hold up and ask yourself some questions, such as—

• *Do I really want forgiveness?*

• *Am I truly sorry for what I did?*

• *Do I simply want to get off the hook quick?*

• *Am I just anxious to finagle this into some fast pleasure?*

• *Am I simply trying to avoid some serious pain?*

There have been times when a guest on *Forgive or Forget* has sought forgiveness without truly being sorry.

Take the young man who came on the show to apologize for cheating on his ex-girlfriend with whom he had a child. He wanted another chance. "I just really want to tell her that I'm truly sorry," he said, "and that she is my soul mate, the only one for me, and I want her to take me back."

As he told his story, it became crystal clear why his ex had quit him.

"How many times have you cheated on her?" I asked.

"Five."

Uh-oh. And it got worse: he had cheated on her with five different women, and with two of the women he'd had a child—and these two children were about the same age.

My heart broke for stud-man's ex, facing the truth out in the open, up on the screen with the world knowing how her fella had dogged her, and people in the audience looking at her as if she's got Dippy Foo Foo stamped on her forehead.

This time girlfriend decided to be fool-no-more, for she was not behind the door. The young man was stunned.

"Yes!" I wanted to shout. "You reap what you sow, young man," I wanted to say. Heartache in. Heartache out.

He broke down and cried. Did I feel sorry for him? A little. I felt sorry that he had been a nincompoop and too slow to change his ways. But his tears did not make me sorry that his ex hadn't walked through the door. I was glad she had found some pride. The audience was like, "You go, girl!" They applauded when stud-man faced that empty door.

"Oh, Mother Love, calm the audience down!" That was my producer freaking out in my ear. "He's *crying,* for heaven's sake!" Didn't I want to snatch that plug out of my ear! I was two seconds from sounding off on that young man. "The more you cry, the less you'll pee," is what I felt like telling him. But, of course, I had to be, well . . . Mother Love.

I've also had to hold my tongue when someone walked through the door with an "All is forgiven and all is forgotten" glow when it was obvious that the person seeking forgiveness wasn't all that sorry for cheating, or lying, or stealing, or whatever. I've wanted to scream, *"Have you lost what's left of your mind?"* I've wanted to shake some sense into the "glow children," rattle them just enough to get them to realize that they should not be doormats, that they deserved better treatment, that until the boneheads were truly sorry, they'd get nothing but the same ole same.

A time or two I have spoken my mind. On one occasion I told a woman who'd given her no-account man a second chance, "You don't need to be that desperate for a man."

STEP 4

Apologize with Sincerity

True confession consists in telling our deed in such a way that our soul is changed in the telling of it.

—Maude Petre

I'd rather have a genuine, heartfelt apology that took twenty years to birth than a lame sorry that came in ten seconds.

A sincere apology is hard to fake unless you are a brilliant actor or a pathological liar. Most people can tell when someone is half-stepping. So come real or don't come at all.

When you show up with a true desire to apologize,

whether or not someone forgives you, your effort will not be in vain. There are no guarantees but there is hope. After all, the act of apologizing frees *you* up.

Better one living word than a hundred dead ones.

—German proverb

If you get the itch to present someone with a washy "Sorry," you need to scratch. A sorry with strings attached—with lots of buts, clauses, conditions, stipulations, and woulda-shoulda-couldas—is a sure sign that you cannot pass GO, that you need to hurry your happy butt back to Step 1.

"I know I did wrong, but after all, you provoked me."

"I'm sorry I screamed like a banshee, but I had PMS and you knew that."

"I apologize for lying about what happened the other night, but in the future I'd appreciate it if you wouldn't press me before I'm ready to speak."

"I admit that what I said was cold, but don't you think you're a little too sensitive?"

No buts. No excuses. That kind of poppycock will not do. A sincere apology doesn't lay blame at the feet of the person from whom you are seeking forgiveness.

Not all explanation is a no-no, however. Sometimes explaining the circumstances is a mark of sincerity and is part of the balm. If, for instance, you were unable to make good on a promise because of unforeseen circumstances (the computer Auntie), sharing this information with the person you've disappointed could be a good move—just so long as you don't fall into the trap of using it to evoke pity.

Apology is a lovely perfume; it can transform the clumsiest moment into a gracious gift.

—Margaret Lee Runbeck

STEP 5

Apologize in a Way That Makes Sense for You

Forethought spares afterthought.

—Amelia E. Barr

The medium might be as important as the message.

If time and space permit, you might opt for a face-to-face. It takes courage to apologize in person, to look people right in the window of their souls and say, "I'm sorry." It takes courage to let the wronged party look straight in your eyes and see you're sorry. Yes, it takes courage to do it, and after you do, you will feel a great relief.

If you're considering a face-to-face, use wisdom: if you know or suspect that the wronged person is hot-tempered, there's no nobility in unnecessarily putting yourself in harm's way. Uh-uh.

It's possible that the person you've wronged lives three thousand miles away. If making a special trip is imperative, you'll know it: something inside will compel you to go. I wager that in most cases it would be a bit much to make a special trek. When this is true, then go on and invest your five or ten cents a minute in the matter.

You may be supremely sincere about your "Sorry," and the person whose forgiveness you seek may be only a bus ride, a block, a room, a cubicle, or a local phone call away. Yet you may be the kind of person who's prone to flub when it comes to speaking from the heart. If this is you, then write the person you've wronged a good old-fashioned letter. Be sure to keep a copy of this letter for your self-improvement archives. Read it from time to time. Remember the journey.

If a face-to-face or a telephone call is impossible or inadvisable, and the very idea of committing your thoughts to paper gives you the sweats or the runs, take advantage of technology: present your apology on an audio- or videotape. If you choose this option, as with a letter, it will be worth your while to keep a copy for yourself.

If you want to do something bolder than all of the above, come to Mother Love—be a guest on *Forgive or Forget* (1-877-APOLOGY).

A thing done at a wrong time should be regarded as not done.

—Sanskrit proverb

Whichever way you choose to apologize, give the apology some thought. As a rule, it's not a good idea to walk up to the person you've harmed or snatch up the phone in the first flush of repentance. Similarly, if you send off a letter or a tape before you've had a chance to sleep on it, you may be setting yourself up for some regrets. Remember: haste makes waste.

Giving your apology some thought doesn't mean obsessing over form and content. While these things matter, if they begin to matter too much, your apology may have degenerated into a vanity act.

Are there occasions when a spontaneous "Sorry" is OK, and perhaps even necessary? Every day. There are all those little blunders we make, in which case, if we've had any home training, we will apologize quickly and with ease—should we step on someone's foot, interrupt someone, sneeze in someone's face, spill grape juice on somebody's carpet, fail to return a phone call, knock somebody down in a rush for a seat on the subway or bus, snap at a subordinate because the boss snapped at us, neglect to say, "Thank you," and so on and so forth ad infinitum. We all do a little messing up in the course of our everyday comings and goings and hanging around.

STEP 6

Be Ready to Make Restitution

The danger with feelings of penitence is that we allow them to take the place of those actions that are its manifestation.

—Elizabeth Cullinan

There's nothing like a deed to back up your words.

If you're sorry for not repaying Betty that $50 she lent you, then hand (or send) her an Uncle Ben along with your apology.

Did you dent the fender of your friend's car and then lie about it? Well, when you fess up, tell your friend to send you the bill for the repair.

"But Mother Love, Betty doesn't really need that fifty dollars."

"But Mother Love, my friend's insurance will pay for the dent, though since it's not a big dent, he probably won't even worry about getting it fixed."

It is not your place to decide whether somebody needs or wants whatever you offer to restore or replace. If the person accepts your apology and declines the repayment, fine. Let that be his or her choice.

Let your restitution be in place when you apologize. Like the woman who came on our show to apologize to her sister for not repaying a loan: along with her apology, she had the first payment. That's called having your act together. (There's no excuse for not having a plan.)

And please don't take a page from Tara's book. She had wrecked the car of her best friend, Tisha. To add insult to injury, she reneged on her promise to pay Tisha's $500 deductible. Tisha ended up losing her car, which meant losing her job. On top of that, she lost a friendship. Tara just dropped Tisha. She moved and left no forwarding address, and when, on two occasions, Tisha ran into her, Tara gave her a bogus phone number. Finally, after two years, Tara got up the gumption to ask Tisha to forgive her.

Tisha, who'd lost so much, was behind the door

and very eager to resume the friendship, all the more so when Tara triple-promised to pay up the $500. Everything was going fine, peaches and cream, until someone in the audience asked Tara, "Would you still give the money if she hadn't forgiven you?"

I was floored when Tara said, "No."

> The truth of the matter is that you always know the right thing to do. The hard part is doing it.
>
> —H. Norman Schwarzkopf

What if the wrong can't be righted? Hmmmm. It happens. You can't unslam a door. You can't grab up gossip and toss it into the deep blue sea. You can't rewind a person's life to childhood and undo emotional, physical, or sexual abuse. You may not have the $50 at the time you are ready to apologize. If your transgression was infidelity, you'd have to be *insane* to think that giving your spouse a free cheat on you is restitution. And what if the bracelet you borrowed from your sister without her permission and then lost was one of a kind? What if the person you wronged is no longer among the living?

He who upsets a thing should know how to
rearrange it.

—Sierra Leone proverb

There are thousands of cases in which one cannot
make exact restitution. Still, some restitution can be
made, and it is up to you to find what that thing is.
Here's a start on brainstorming.

- *If your sister's bracelet was one of a kind, replace it
  with something comparable, or give her the money to
  make such a purchase.*

- *If you've abused a child or a grown person, you can
  donate your time or some cash (or both) to an
  organization that aids victims of abuse.*

- *If the matter revolves around money, and the person
  to whom you are indebted declines the money, give
  him or her a gift that fits. This gift might be something
  store-bought (flowers, a plant, a scarf, a CD, or this
  book) or something homemade (a cake, a pie, a
  poem). It doesn't have to match dollar for dollar; it's
  the thought that counts. So put some thought into it.*

· *If the person you wronged is deceased, make restitution to the next of kin. That's what one of our guests did, a young woman who had stolen from her aunt. By the time this young woman dealt with what she had done, Auntie was dead, so she made amends to her cousin, Auntie's daughter. (And if there is no next of kin, do a stranger a good deed.)*

There's lots of room to be creative when making restitution. If you're stumped at first and you are genuinely sorry, the appropriate thing will make itself known to you. And always remember that—as with acknowledging wrongdoing, being repentant, and offering an apology—making restitution is as much a good deed to ourselves as it is to the person we wronged, because restitution is part of taking responsibility for what we've done, and when we take responsibility, we win the battle.

Last thing: bear in mind that if tangible restitution proves elusive, in Step 8 you'll find the ultimate restitution.

STEP 7

Prepare Yourself for Any Outcome

Life is a gamble, a chance, a mere guess. Cast a line and reel in a splendid rainbow trout or a slippery eel.

—Mourning Dove

Yes, for every action, there is a reaction.

One of the biggest hindrances to apologizing is fear of rejection: a flat-out *"Forget it!"*—or worse. Often, before we proffer our apology, we script a horror movie and play it repeatedly in our minds.

"What if she says she'll never speak to me again?"

"What if he leaves me?"

"What if other people think I'm going soft, becoming a wimp?"

"What if she screams and hollers at me?"

"What if they tell everybody what I did?"

These what-ifs could very well happen, but obsessing on the negative only immobilizes us, undermining our desire to do the right thing.

If we are genuine about wanting to right our lives, we ought not fret about the outcome. We ought only prepare ourselves as best we can for any eventuality.

You ought to prepare for things like—

"I can't see my way to forgive you *ever*."

"I appreciate your apology, but in all honesty, it's going to take time for me to truly forgive you."

"I forgive you, but don't you ever come within two feet of me—even if I'm on fire!"

"I accept your apology and bear you no malice. However, I no longer want to have any kind of relationship with you."

That last one brings to mind Tyon and Tish. These two were high school sweethearts, each the other one's first love in a true romance that didn't include sex. These lovebirds wanted to wait.

Well, off they went to college, and things fell apart. The breaking point was a young lady who set her sights on Tyon. She and Tyon were in his room one day when—"One thing led to another" was how Tyon (predictably) summed it up.

When Tish found out about Tyon's tryst, she was hurt and she was angry. Making matters worse, the young lady who seduced Tyon was going out with his cousin, and she was also, allegedly, a friend of Tish. After Tyon's betrayal, whenever Tish and Tyon's paths crossed, butter wouldn't melt in Tish's mouth.

Tyon came to miss Tish. They had known each other since they were children. Before they were sweethearts, they had been best friends. Tyon wasn't holding out much hope that he and Tish could be sweethearts again, but he was hoping that they could return to being friends. So he came on *Forgive or Forget* to tell his story and to beg Tish's pardon.

I have to give the young man credit: in telling his story, he didn't make excuses, but rather, he said straight-up that he was a virgin at the time and that he had let his hormones get the better of him. He admitted (though it took a little prodding from Mother Love) that he never should have let that young lady into his room, never should have accommodated her when she asked him to turn on his black light, never should have let her sit so close beside him on the bed, never should have let her start picking some lint off his face, stroking his face in the process, and increasing the likelihood that one thing would lead to another.

I don't think there was anybody in the audience who didn't think Tyon wasn't for real when he said he was sorry—sorry for letting lust get the better of him, sorry for hurting Tish. There were more than a few audience members who were rooting for Tyon and Tish to get back together.

Did they? Was Tish behind the door? Was she prepared to let the past be the past? Was she ready to start anew with Tyon?

When the door swung open, Tish was there all right. Tyon's smile could have fired a rocket, and Tish looked bewildered.

She forgave him, yes. And yes, she said that from then on she wouldn't be igging him when she saw him. She also said that she no longer wanted to have a relationship with him, not even a friendship.

Hmmmm. Why did she say she was forgiving him?

"The God in me won't allow me to be rude to him for the rest of my life," Tish strongly and softly explained.

In forgiving Tyon, Tish wasn't just being gracious toward him. She was also cleansing herself from malice and spite, and getting on with her life. Her honesty was most commendable.

What about Tyon?

He was hurt that Tish rejected his offer of a new friendship. The glow he had when he saw Tish behind the door began to fade as closure came. You could see he was doing everything in his power to keep his chin up. Didn't always work, though.

Life gives us what we need when we need it. Receiving what it gives us is a whole other thing.

—Pam Houston

In the end, Tyon didn't fight the bad news. He didn't argue with Tish. He didn't trip into a whiny "But I *said* I was sorry. What do you mean you don't want to be my friend!" Instead, he began the process of accepting Tish's reality. He chose to see the glass as half full, and he chose to be grateful for that.

If someone is not willing to forgive you, accept it as a lesson learned—a strong reminder that your words and actions can cause great injury and sometimes the ending won't be so happily-ever-after.

On the other hand . . .

It's quite possible that your apology will be met with not only forgiveness, but also with praise and maybe a bonus to boot—

"Of course I forgive you! And we need to find some way to celebrate our new beginning."

"Thank you, thank you. You've made my day!"

"Your courage to apologize is an inspiration—encouraging me to deal with the apologies I owe a few folks."

"I know it took a lot for you to fess up and come clean. I honor that. What's more, I am not going to press charges and I'll nix the restraining order."

> There are times when life surprises one, and anything may happen, even what one had hoped for.
>
> —Ellen Glasgow

Yes, your sincere apology may get you out of a jam. A broken or strained marriage may be mended. You may be rehired on a job. A membership on a sports team or in a club may be restored. Gone may be the days of grimaces from an acquaintance.

If, after you've made your apology and act of restitution, good things flow from others to you, be sure to savor this and, most important, be humble.

Whichever way things go, when you say, "I'm sorry," and make restitution, you will be strengthened, renewed, and restored.

STEP 8

Commit to Change Your Ways

Clarity is not a thought process but a way of life.

—Keorapetse Kgositsile

If you want a good life, try to understand your mistakes and vow never to repeat them. If your transgression, faux pas, mistake—whatever—was a one-time affair, yes, file it, but do not forget it. Don't forget the harm you caused. Don't forget the price you paid (from the guilt to the restitution), and don't forget the price someone else paid. While not dwelling on these things, you need to remember them in case you

are ever tempted to repeat the offense. Let the memo-
ries be your internal STOP sign.

Take Ann, who came on *Forgive or Forget* to apologize to her friend Robert for fixing him up with a
friend of hers. Ann had meant well, but as it turned
out, she didn't know her friend as well as she thought
she did: this friend turned out to be crazy-possessive
of Robert (we're talking stalker-ville here) and almost
drove him out of his mind. I bet Ann will think long
and hard before she ever plays matchmaker again.
(And Robert forgave her.)

Don't look where you fell, but where you slipped.

—Liberian proverb

If your offense is something you've done often,
then you'll have more work to do. Get to the root of
your problem. Only then will you begin to repair
what's really wrong. The work you do on this will not
only help you get past the wrong; it will also open the
door to new, positive opportunities in your world—in
your finances, on your job, in your friendships, in
your romantic life.

Some people don't vow to change unless they are forgiven. Others make the commitment before they ask for forgiveness. These people, you have to cheer them. Like Bruce, who came on the show to apologize to his ex-girlfriend Susan for being physically and emotionally abusive. He wanted her to forgive him and he wanted her to take him back. And he wasn't offering her just the same old Bruce: by the time he came on the show, Bruce was already in anger management courses.

Or take Debbie. Her daughter, Keesha, came on the show to prod Debbie into recognizing the horrors she'd laid on Keesha and her fourteen-year-old brother, Jerry, as a consequence of her nine-year addiction to crack-cocaine. Keesha was especially worried about her brother, who was beginning to become enamored with thug life.

To talk goodness is not good—only to do it is.

—Chinese proverb

Keesha wanted to have the good relationship she once had with her mother. She wanted to forgive her

mother for the nine-year nightmare. But Keesha was
not going to surrender herself and get her hopes up
high for some long-overdue mother love from Debbie
unless Debbie apologized for her behavior and also
declared that she was serious about seeking help (and
not do as she'd done before: slick her way out of a
rehab center and later claim that she could get clean
on her own).

Debbie was behind the door. As mother and
daughter took their place together on the sofa, I didn't
know whose tears were flowing fastest. Debbie was
sorry. Debbie was so, so, very sorry. With a strength
and poise I've rarely seen in one so young, Keesha
forcefully, but without malice or disrespect, said to
her mother, "It's been *hard*. . . . I'm sick of having to
play mother to your child. I'm sick of having to basically babysit you too." Keesha went on to talk about
the times when she dared not watch the news
"because I didn't know if it was going to be you
found dead next."

Debbie's son, Jerry, was there in the audience rooting
for his mother. "Mommy, I just wish you would just go
to the rehab," he said. "I don't want you out there in the
street like that. That's not the right lifestyle for you.
You're better than that." Remembering Keesha's con-
cern about Jerry getting sweet on the streets, I gave this

precious soon-to-be-man a hug and reminded him, "And you can do better too."

Sow an act and you reap a habit; sow a habit and you reap a character; sow a character and you reap a destiny.

—Frances E. Willard

Debbie's remorse and regret were so apparent, she surely did seem ready to become that better person her children believed in and came on our show to fight for. I had hoped that Debbie would be ready to fight her addiction, and being the optimists that we are at *Forgive or Forget*, we had put things in place to help Debbie take that next step if she so chose. I wasn't going to let that woman leave the show with only her promise to hold onto, oh no. I had Andrea Piggott in the audience, the assistant director of a substance abuse treatment center up in New England where Debbie and her children lived.

The first thing Ms. Piggott did was commend Debbie for having the courage to deal with her problem. Then she proceeded to run down the various services her center offered. When I asked how long it would take to get Debbie into the program, Piggott said, "We can set Debbie up immediately." Then, directly to Debbie, she said, "If you're willing, we'll do whatever it takes to get you the treatment you need."

Keesha and Jerry and Debbie—this little family was on the road to being whole again.

Hold onto these examples, and know that heaven smiles mightily on the recovering liar, thief, crank, batterer, racist, bully, shrew, gossip, adulterer, and fink. And you must remember this: NOT REPEATING A WRONG IS THE ULTIMATE RESTITUTION!

Remember President Clinton's statement following his acquittal on charges of perjury and obstruction of justice? He was subdued, diplomatic, presidential, and true to the moratorium on gloating we'd heard about. But only a Bo-Bo with two left feet could think that the man wasn't at least a wee bit peeved with those Republicans who beat the drum for his ouster (not to mention Kenneth Starr).

Clinton's statement was brief and his exit to be quick and painless, but then a beat after he turned from the microphone, the Snapdragon, Sam Donaldson, called out, "In your heart, can you forgive and forget?"

Clinton flinched and came to a halt. He turned back with a fair amount of heat. Then he seemed to mellow. One could only wonder if in those few seconds between the question and his answer, all the apologies he had offered for his "inappropriate behavior"—to his wife, his child, his staff, the American people, Buddy—raced through his psyche.

With a little more humility on his face and more light than heat, Clinton answered, "I believe that any person who asks for forgiveness has to be prepared to give it."

I know some citizens figured that Clinton was just being coy, cagey, all-politics-all-the-time. I didn't allow my mind to go down that road. Instead, I savored those words because they are good words.

PART III

Forgiveness is the economy of the heart. . . .
Forgiveness saves the expense of anger,
the cost of hatred, the waste of spirits.
—Hannah More

To err is human; to forgive, divine.
—Alexander Pope

Blessed are the merciful: for they shall obtain mercy.
—Jesus

When the human mind is once completely under the dominion of pride and selfishness, the reasoning faculties are inverted if not subverted.

—Frederick Douglass

People who are unforgiving have no sense of ethics, no sense of compassion, no sense of reality—no sense, period. They are cramped, crippled souls living under the illusion that their vindictive spirit, their stockpile of rage and wrath, makes them a victor and keeps them strong, in control, in charge. Such people are bone-heads. They would disagree, of course, because they think they are smart, very smart. Indeed, they are too smart, and as the saying goes, "Too smart is stupid."

These too-smart people don't know anything about the power of love—the fact that tenderness, charity, and mercy have innumerable and often intangible rewards. These too-smart people do not understand that anger, the taproot of revenge, blocks blessings and breeds destruction. In short, these too-smart people do not understand the KISS principle ("Keep It Simple, Stupid").

> Anger is often more hurtful than the injury that caused it.
>
> —English proverb

A self-centered person cannot forgive, because forgiveness is *giving*. It's doing a wrongdoer a good turn. For starters:

- *When you forgive, you help those who wronged you get on with their lives and lead them more productively and creatively.*

- *When you forgive, you inspire others to be forgiving—those who wronged you and those who are watching you from afar or up close.*

You also do yourself a good turn when you forgive.

- *When you forgive, you get relief from the pain an offense has caused you, and your wound begins to heal.*

- *When you forgive, you free yourself of a burden, a problem, and a bad memory's stifle on your soul.*

- *When you forgive, you can strike off from your life-list another bit of unfinished business, a loose end.*

- *When you forgive, you advance your goal of doing your life better day by day, day after day.*

- *When you forgive, you increase the likelihood that you will be forgiven when you need an open, understanding heart.*

- *When you forgive, you can better concentrate on rebuilding relationships: if someone who wronged you matters to you, the two of you can get on with the business of loving. If your grudge against someone has negatively affected others who are important to you, you can start fresh by asking their forgiveness.*

- *When you forgive, you improve your overall mental/emotional/spiritual health, for according to*

the National Institute of Healthcare Research, the act
of forgiveness is linked to lower depression and
anxiety; it's a self-esteem booster.

The practice of forgiveness is our most important
contribution to the healing of the world.

—Marianne Williamson

Doesn't this stuff sound good? Don't you want some
of it? If you answered in the affirmative, Mother Love
hopes you take to heart what follows on forgiving.

STEP #1

Renounce Revenge

Revenge is the poor delight of little minds.

—Juvenal

You cannot forgive if you are vengeful. It's that simple. So before you can think about forgiving, you must renounce revenge.

Revenge is plain wrong, and as I reminded readers in Part II, two wrongs—you know the rest. Therefore, if someone hits you, you must refrain from striking back (or paying someone else to do it) unless it's in self-defense. And so it goes for other injuries: the one stolen from ought not steal from the thief; the one cheated on ought not have a fling or a full-blown affair; those who have been slandered ought not spread lies and unflattering truths about the people who soiled their reputations.

To take revenge is often to sacrifice oneself.

—Bakongo proverb

We also ought not commit what we think will be an equivalent wrong, such as egging the car of a lover who callously dumped you, or siccing the IRS on someone who cheated you, or sabotaging the work- or play-related plans of someone who bad-mouthed you. If you do such things, you become a vandal, or a snitch, or a killjoy. Soon you could be a serious danger.

Men regard it as their right to return evil for evil— and if they cannot, feel they have lost their liberty.

—Aristotle

What's behind revenge? It's the notion that those who have wronged you should suffer and that you deserve to participate in their suffering. It's a desire to see someone shackled to a wall in a dungeon, with you as the head guard. I'm not saying that there shouldn't be consequences and sometimes even punishment for wrongdoing. I'm merely stressing that revenge is a perversion. It's also a delusion: we can't ever really revenge a wrong. Our efforts to do so (even if "successful") only put us in lockdown.

Revenge has no more quenching effect on emotions than salt water has on thirst.

— Walter Weckler

Not avenging a wrong is the endgame. If you manage this, you have accomplished a lot. There's more, however: namely, not even wanting to get revenge. This is the really hard part and the ultimate triumph. If you've not been at it much, it will take some time; it will take some work.

As the wound inflames the finger, so the thought inflames the mind.

—Ethiopian proverb

Not wanting to retaliate takes *you* seriously talking to *you* and telling yourself to banish all fantasies of payback. If revenge fantasies cross your mind, don't panic, don't think you're an evil, unredeemable person, for control of our thought life is no easy feat. It's very hard to forget that you had to call your sister about the $975 she borrowed—money you really didn't have to lend, money she promised to pay back two Fridays ago—and that now she won't even return your calls. It takes grace not to rage, and grace takes practice.

Controlling your thought life requires reminding yourself that the issue is not what thoughts come to you, but how you handle thoughts. Should some act of revenge pop into your head, all you need do is not entertain it. The next wicked concoction should leave more quickly—and the next, and the next, until such ugly thoughts may one day not even know where to find you.

Watch out too for vicarious, secondhand revenge: rejoicing when a calamity strikes someone who injured you. This brings to mind a story a friend told me about two women she knows: one, whom I'll call Julia, and the other, whom I'll call Yvonne. Julia and Yvonne were once very close friends, but their close friendship ended when Julia confronted Yvonne about her feelings that Yvonne had betrayed her in a business matter. Yvonne basically blew Julia off; she could not concede that she'd done anything wrong.

Julia quit the friendship. To her credit, she never did anything to harm Yvonne personally or professionally; however, she hung onto a grudge. Her anger and resentment became quite apparent when Yvonne's husband left her: when Julia called my friend with Yvonne's bad news, "The glee in her voice was almost sickening," my friend said. What saddened my friend was that Julia, a sincere Christian, didn't seem to be aware that she was rejoicing over Yvonne's misfortune.

My friend's postscript to this story was this: a few months after Julia's gloat over Yvonne's collapsed marriage, my friend (also a Christian) heard that someone who'd cheated her out of some money had suffered a business loss. "Before I knew it," said my friend, "out of my mouth flew 'Good for him!'" Yes, this business of renouncing vicarious revenge does not come easy, not even for those who know better.

You'll know you're not free of the Revenge Monster if, when something wonderful happens to someone who wronged you, you are galled, appalled, and fit to be tied. You put yourself through these changes because you feel that the person has gotten off, gotten over. The truth is that wrongdoers who do not repent and make amends do pay. (Remember this: you may get by, but you won't get away.) Such people pay in ways you cannot imagine and in ways you may never get wind of—even when they are prospering on the surface.

It is never wise to seek or wish for another's misfortune. If malice or envy were tangible and had a shape, it would be the shape of a boomerang.

—Charley Reese

One way to exorcize a vengeful spirit is to think about the intentional and accidental wrongs you've committed. As you scroll down the list, ask yourself what your life might be like (or if you'd even have a life) if everyone you wronged exacted revenge on you—directly, or indirectly by harming your loved ones. Consider too how you would feel if everyone you ever wronged celebrated (together!) if you lost a job, fell ill, lost a loved one, or suffered some other tragedy. And what if this same crowd launched a hissing campaign when you came into some good fortune or had a triumph? Perhaps some of this stuff has happened to you. How did it make you feel?

I imagine one of the reasons people cling to their hates so stubbornly is because they sense, once hate is gone, they will be forced to deal with pain.

—James Baldwin

Remember this too: if you do not let go of the urge for revenge, not only will you be unable to forgive, but you're liable to land in a deep sea of hatred, which is an unsafe place to be (even if you can swim). I tell you no lie: people get sick and people lose their minds behind harboring revenge and hatred.

Also, vengeful people have an odor about them. Those who hide their sour soul don't have many friends and know little up close love. No matter how you try to perfume it, if you're walking around with longings for revenge, perceptive people will vibe in on it. They'll find you somewhat distasteful. Maybe they won't be able to put their finger on it, but they just won't like your "scent." This strange knowing may very well prompt people to keep you at arms' length and turn you down or overlook you for promotions, recommendations, gifts, loans, dates, the time of day.

Living well is the best revenge.

—George Herbert

Renouncing revenge isn't just about avoiding pain and doom. There are benefits, blessings. Energy invested in getting back at someone or fantasizing about it can be much better spent. If you're not plotting pay-back, you're freed up to strategize on how you can improve your finances, your work life, your diet, your home life, your babies—pick a life, get on with life, enjoy your life!

STEP #2

Don't Worry About the Negative Vibers

Insistent advice may develop into interference, and interference, someone has said, is the hind hoof of the devil.

—Carolyn Wells

Often people fail to forgive because they are more concerned about others thinking they're weak than they are about freeing and cleansing themselves.

There you are, clear about the need to forgive and ready to reap the bounty. Then you make your intentions known to a certain kind of person and you get hit with—

"Have you lost your mind? How can you even think of forgiving them after what they've done to you?"

Or . . .

"I wouldn't forgive him for breathing!"

Or . . .

"For-*give*? The only thing I'd *give* her is my foot up her—"

The moon does not trouble itself about the howling of dogs.

—Italian proverb

Never listen to staunch unforgivers or bearers of bitterness. Such people will only bring you down, so far down that you'll have to look up to see the bottom.

Only the brave know how to forgive; it is the most refined and generous pitch of virtue human nature can strive at.

—Laurence Sterne

When you decide to forge ahead with forgiving, against the advice of negative people, be prepared for these nimrods to trash you worse than you ever thought of trashing the person who dogged you out. These bubbleheads may find your forgiving spirit a frailty. They may feel betrayed in some way. What's behind all this?

Because knuckleheads tend to be pessimistic about everything, they may think that in forgiving, you're setting yourself up to be taken advantage of (and that's *their* job). Misery loving company may also be a factor—along with the fact that folks often revile those who have the courage to do what they fear to do: people in darkness have a tendency to resent those who set their sights on the light.

You assure them that you're using both your head and your heart, and maybe no matter what you say you're still met with opposition and pressure to hold a grudge. Should this happen, it could be a good thing—just the push you need to rethink your association with these folks.

For a while, my husband (then boyfriend) and I split up. (Can you believe it, given how much I talk about him on the show and how highly I regard him?) It was awful. He didn't want to see me, talk to me, love me. He was tired of my ambitions, my pipe dreams of stardom, my voice, my hair—my everything. I couldn't seem to make him happy, but I knew we were right for one another. I saw in my soul the life we have now. But he left us, our little boy and me. I was crushed but I had to move forward. I had to keep dreaming, keep believing.

I cried and cried and tried and tried and cried and tried. Nothing worked. To make matters worse, everyone around me—my sisters, my mother, my girlfriends, every old boyfriend—had something to say. It was as if my love life had been broadcast on the six o'clock news and I'd asked for the viewers' responses.

"We told you he was no good, and there you was all wrapped up into him, doing everything—cooking, cleaning, washing, wifing, with no ring, no name, no plans, no future."

He wanted to "find" himself. "I'm the other half of you, and you me," I'd tell him.

I kept trying, praying, and forgiving. Everybody called me stupid, whipped, fool.

And I was like, "But—"

And they—"You're too good for him!"

And I was like, "But—"

And they—"You put your heart and soul into him and he left you!"

And I was like, "But—"

They just beat me up, every single day. I couldn't even call anybody and tell them my heart was broken.

Most every woman I knew had a real negative attitude about men. "All men are dogs!" they'd say.

Well, after my man "found" himself, he apologized with all his heart, his whole being. One day he showed up at my door and told me to pack my stuff and move to his house by 5 P.M. I (at first) refused because I was still grieving his leaving.

"You will see a change in me," he vowed. "Our love and our life with our son will be true and dear."

I wanted to go right then, and I had to hear—

"Don't take him back!"

"Don't forgive him!"

"Don't speak to him!"

"Don't love him!"

My man had to brave negative vibers too. More than a few of his friends and kin told him he was a jerk for apologizing to me. "That's a *woman*. You don't owe her spit. You the boss." That, from menfolks. As for the womenfolk—"She won't *ever* be good enough for you! She's loud, fat, and too opinionated."

Trust yourself. Think for yourself. Act for yourself. Speak for yourself. Be yourself. Imitation is suicide.

—Marva Collins

We decided, after viewing all our faults (his quiet, arrogant, and stubborn ways and my fat, loud, and opinionated self)—we decided we didn't want to be miserable. We are right for each other. Period! Forgiving him for leaving me was the best thing I ever did for myself, our son, our love.

It gives me pleasure to say that all my sisters who gave me grief for getting back with my man later apologized (and forgave their men their nonsense). My husband's friends and kin came to accept me as his queen. As for our prince, he's still very happy with both of us.

STEP #3

Don't Confuse Revenge with Restitution

Only lies and evil come from letting people off.

—Iris Murdoch

If a person's apology includes restitution or some peace offering, accept it. All the way around, that's generally the good and gracious thing to do. It helps you and the other person wipe the slate clean, close the book, turn the page, come to closure, begin anew.

Not accepting a tangible sign of "I'm sorry" is often more a matter of false modesty than mercy, so check yourself before you decline the offering. Is your "Oh, that's not necessary" for real? Would you really like to have—or could you really use—the money repaid, the camera replaced, the botched paint job made right? Would that piece of jewelry, the tickets to a show, the book, the dinner, the whatever—would that token of remorse give you pleasure? If yes, then what's up with "Oh, that's not necessary"? Do you think that makes you appear noble? If this is the case, you may very well need to accept the restitution so as not to give ground to false pride. And when you do, please don't coo, "Oh, you shouldn't have."

What if your heart is in a good place? What if you're not a phony? What if you suspect or know that restitution will put the person in a bind? Wouldn't it be uncharitable to accept it? Sometimes.

Let's say Uncle Bootsie's replacement of a stolen item (which he hocked) will result in his falling behind on rent or another pressing debt. Here the wise thing to do would be to forfeit the restitution or at least work out a compassionate timetable. If you put Uncle Bootsie between a rock and a hard place, you may instigate his temptation to steal again from somebody else (a literal robbing of Peter to pay Paul).

On the other hand, if the restitution won't have a disastrous effect on Uncle Bootsie but may only pinch, you could be doing him a disservice if you decline it. Uncle Bootsie may very much need to feel the pinch because he may need a "receipt" for a life lesson. Some people never get any sense unless they pay for it. As one of my "world famous" friends always says, "Ain't nothing like some bought sense." When our righting of a wrong includes money out of our pocket or sweat from our brow, we're more apt to do everything in our power not to repeat the transgression. Haven't you noticed that kids who never have to pay for windows their baseballs have shattered shatter a lot of windows? Haven't you noticed that folks who get busted, and therefore fined, by the IRS are more likely to cease and desist from cheating on their income tax returns? Haven't you ever heard of noncareer criminals taking more pains to be lawabiding after they've spent some time in jail?

Nothing strengthens the judgment and quickens the conscience like individual responsibility.

—Elizabeth Cady Stanton

Here's another dilemma many have found themselves in: what if the person offers a sincere apology but doesn't mention restitution? Do you bring it up?

Is doing so crass, brash, rude, tacky, and on top of that, rubbing salt in a wound? Again, it depends on the situation. Sometimes bringing up restitution would be an exercise in futility. You may know, for example, that your little sister Tamara is living on borrowed money as it is and wouldn't be able to repay the loan for years. Or you may know that Brother's running buddy, Leon, has neither the time nor the skill to redo—properly—the house painting job he botched. Then again, if you think restitution is doable, totally or in part, why not bring it up? Remember: you may need to fend off false modesty, and Tamara and Leon may need to "buy some sense."

Restitution can be a tangly thing. There's no one-size-fits-all blanket policy. If you're in the forgiveness mode, wisdom and common sense will come to your rescue case by case. Let your conscience be your guide. As I said earlier, I assume you have a conscience. Otherwise you wouldn't be reading this.

STEP #4

Be Wise About "Why?"

We are such curious creatures. When we've been wronged, nine times out of ten we feel compelled to know and understand why someone did what they did. *"Why? Why? Why? Why? Why?"* is our inner cry, and sometimes we shout it out *real* loud.

Sometimes people wrong you and you haven't a clue about the cause. Perhaps you replay the scene repeatedly. Perhaps you search your memory for previous dealings with that person, hoping to find a key. Perhaps you snoop. All because you're on fire to figure out what was behind the theft, the betrayal, the lie, the abandonment. All because you think that your having this information is critical to closure. *"Was it something I did?"* we often wonder.

Sometimes you will know why someone wronged you. You may know, for instance, that your brother's girlfriend stole from you because she's a drug addict. You may know that your cousin lied to you because he's a chronic liar. You may know that your boyfriend picked a fight with you because he wanted to break up with you but didn't know how to do it like a grown-up. You may know that Mutt and Jeff, your otherwise kindly, sensitive coworkers, laughed loud at jokes particularly offensive to you because they are sheep and unable not to "go with the flow."

Whether or not you know why somebody wronged you, the question is, Do you ask that somebody "Why?"

It depends. Let your decision rest on honest answers to the following questions.

Will an explanation change anything?

It could. If Stanley Steele stole from you because of an addiction about which you know zip, your knowledge of his problem can improve your future dealings with him. Until he is clean, you know better than to leave cash or anything else that's an easy swipe in plain sight when he's around. If Zelda, who went off on you, is bipolar, paranoid-schizophrenic, or suffering from some other mental illness, you'll know that you can't take her episodes of rage personally. Similarly, neighbor Mabel may have been unkind to you because she is under some serious stress (death of a loved one, divorce, loss of a job, a kid in the slammer). Your having this information should speed up the peace between the two of you.

Bear in mind also that a lot of offenses are sparked by misinformation and lies. Gladys may have done something to you in retaliation for some wrong she thought you'd committed. Or you may have unwittingly done something that provoked her to pay you back. Gladys's act of revenge is certainly not excusable, but being aware of the motivation would enable you to set the record straight and stop any more revenge that might be heading your way. (Note: Because revengers rarely apologize, you will probably not get a chance to ask "Why?" unless you seek an apology. So be sure not to skip Step 5.)

It ain't so much what people don't know that hurts as what they know that ain't so.

—Artemus Ward

Perhaps the most heart-wrenching "Why?" comes from people who were abandoned by a parent. Too often children think there was something wrong with them that made a parent leave and never look back. Sometimes all the questioning and explaining in the world doesn't help, because what the abandoned person really wants to know is, "Have I at least been on your mind all these years?" If child and parent are reunited, along with that question there's this one: "Will you love me now?"

Will "Why?" bring more agony to the person who offended you than comfort to you?

There are inquiries which are a sort of moral burglary.

—Katharine Fullerton Gerould

Anyone who offers you a genuine apology has already gone through a lot. Pride has been swallowed. Fear of retribution has been conquered. Soul-searching has occurred and may still be going on. Dealing with this reality could cause a person great pain or embarrassment. Too much questioning might even induce the person to commit another transgression (like lie).

It's also possible that giving you an explanation would require that person to tell you somebody else's business that's none of your business.

Are you sure the person knows why?

Reasons are one thing, motives another.

—Charles S. Johnson

Often even the sincerely sorry don't know why they did such-and-such. They may have total recall of the trigger and the sequence of events, but they don't know what's at the root (though they may be working on it). If you push the issue, you won't get a satisfactory answer, and this will only frustrate you.

Do you really just want to see the person squirm?

Sometimes a "Why?" isn't really a question but a beat-down. If you catch yourself relishing the chance to see someone squirm under your interrogation, then you aren't ready to forgive and you need to revisit Step 1.

It often happens that a guest on *Forgive or Forget* receives forgiveness, but then, strangely, the forgiver starts to pester for an explanation, which looks a lot to me like spoiling for a fight.

I thought Michael was about to barrel down that road after he forgave his ex-girlfriend Chandra, who had chumped their relationship by having a one-night stand. After Chandra lost Michael, she realized that he was all the man and the only man she wanted. Along with her apology, there was a come-back-to-me plea.

At the top of the segment and while still backstage, Michael heard Chandra tell Mother Love and the audience (along with everybody else who was tuned in) how she fell into the trap of a cheat. She had put on pounds she couldn't shake, and this plunged her into depression, insecurity, and a whine that Michael wasn't paying her enough attention. She'd become a mess. Chandra wasn't making excuses, oh, no. "I was really unhappy with myself and I took it out on him," she admitted. As I said, Michael heard all this while he was backstage. Yet, after he came through the door, forgiving Chandra, he proceeded to ask her to explain why she had cheated on him. He wanted to know why she didn't try another solution to her self-esteem problem.

I wanted to tell Michael, "Back off, buddy." I had the feeling he just wanted to see Chandra tap-dance for him. I thought the young woman was going to crumble up as she searched for an answer.

"I can't explain, Mike," Chandra finally said. "I was not in a right state of mind."

Michael pressed a little more, and then—"I really do believe that she regrets it," he said, and thankfully, he shut up about the "Why?"

Do you already know why but feel the need to let the person know that you know?

If letting people know that you know why they did something is going to help them reach a quicker liberation from guilt and anguish, you should at least have the compassion not to beat around the bush and pretend you don't know the answer to "Why?" Tell them straight out that you know why the deed was done.

If you want someone to know that you can answer the "Why?" because you think this will make you look wise, or on top of things, or less of a sucker, then you should find a hobby, because obviously you have too much time on your hands.

STEP #5

You May Need to Ask for an Apology

Sometimes the mountain must go to Mohammed.

Yes, that's right. There are times when the wronged party is the one who needs to reach out and ask for an apology.

"Say what?" you say. "If that sorry son-of-a-biscuit-eater doesn't have the decency to come to me and—"

Just hold on a minute.

Haven't you ever heard of sins of omission? Haven't you heard of misunderstandings, accidents, mistakes, oversights? Haven't you ever heard of obliviousness?

Forgiveness is the act of admitting we are like other people.

—Christina Baldwin

Let me put this another way: are you certain that you've never unwittingly injured someone? Think about it. Think about it some more. When you're finished thinking, I believe you'll concede that the same thing can and has happened to others.

We should recognize that everybody is capable of making a mistake, and we should not raise any more hell about somebody else's mistake than we expect to be raised when we make one. Who does not make mistakes? Who is not limited? Everybody but God.

—Duke Ellington

Countless times I've observed or heard about a situation where somebody was harboring hurt and spending precious energy being furious with another person over an offense, and all the while the victim was stewing, the culprit was tootling around totally clueless. Sometimes the matter escalated into an absolutely unnecessary mess, a monster. Sometimes the hurt graduated to hatred—all because the victim didn't have the courage, the good sense, the mercy, to

talk things over with the culprit. Many good relationships have frayed or disintegrated because of non-
communication. What a shame. What a miserable
waste.

If someone you care about or have to deal with a lot
(as on a job) has hurt you in some way, and you haven't
received an apology, consider taking the first step.

Picture this: imagine that you have a mentally disabled brother, and a coworker does a whole routine
of "retard" jokes in your presence. You are offended.
You are angry. You begin to think all manner of terrible things about this coworker. Then . . .

One day you say to that coworker, "Remember the
other day when you were telling those 'retard' jokes?
Well, I feel that was really tasteless and especially
cruel what with my brother being mentally disabled."

Perhaps there's a pause. Perhaps your coworker
frowns. Or maybe he sighs. Then you hear, "Oh, I'm
terribly sorry. I didn't know."

Perhaps you say, "I thought you did."

"Honest. I had no idea . . . but, well . . . come to
think of it, even if you hadn't been there, still it was in
poor taste and . . . just plain . . . wrong."

In this scenario, the air is quickly cleared. What's
more, your coworker has some new information that
he can really use—as in "Won't do that again."

What about you? First of all, you'll feel a heck of a lot better. You'll also stop demonizing that coworker. In the future, you'll make the move sooner to clear the air, won't you?

Of course it's possible that things won't turn out so oola-la-la-ooh. Just as when we apologize, when we ask for an apology we have to be ready for any outcome.

Let's return to our hypothetical about your coworker's offensive jokes. It's possible that instead of contrition, you'll get this: "For crying out loud, I was only joking. Get over it." If this happens, all is not lost. Consider this: at least you will have gained some new insights into your coworker's character and temperament. You have learned that he is more rude and insensitive than you imagined.

Don't let this scenario scare you off from letting people know that they've hurt you. Don't assume the worst of everybody. Don't shortchange your friends, family, neighbors, and strangers by not giving them the benefit of the doubt and thereby rob them of an opportunity to make positive change. I know that I'm very glad a woman named Sierra from Arizona pulled my coattail about something I said during a show that aired at the top of 1999: I referred to someone as an "Indian giver."

Shortly after this show aired, we received an E-mail from Sierra about my use of that term. Sierra's E-mail read in part:

> *I am a Yavapai-Apache Indian. I've grown up hearing the phrase and it hurt because it is referring to my heritage, my people, in a way that is demeaning. I am sure Mother Love was just repeating something she had heard all of her life.*

Yes, I sure did and I sure had. Sierra went on to say:

> *My hope is that she will read this note and choose other words to make her point.*

A few days after receiving it, at the close of a show, I read Sierra's E-mail to my audience and to viewers, apologizing to Sierra and to everyone else who may have taken offense at my use of a stupid (and ahistorical) term. I remain grateful to Sierra for encouraging me to do something I believe in and have been practicing "to choose other words."

Just think, had Sierra written me off as a nimrod, she never would have done the stand-up thing—never would have sent that E-mail. Had she not done so, I might never have reflected on my unfortunate choice of words. I certainly wouldn't have had a golden opportunity to practice, right on the air, what I preach about apologizing, and in so doing move others—in the audience and in front of the tube—to be more aware and to choose their words carefully—about Native Americans, about African-Americans, about European Americans, about all of us. So not only should you never underestimate the power of forgiveness, you should also never underestimate the power of communicating with someone about an offense. Doing this can have far-reaching, wonderful consequences. I think the same applies to sins of commission.

"Wait a minute," you may be thinking. "Is Mother Love saying that I should consider asking for an apology when I know as well as I know my own name that Kirby is not clueless and knows *precisely* what he did?" Yes, that's *precisely* what I'm saying.

If you risk nothing, then you risk everything.

—Geena Davis

Let's face it, not everyone who has wronged you has heard Mother Love's or anybody else's counsel on seeking forgiveness. Many who have, struggle like heck to heed it. In such cases, "the strong ought to bear the infirmities of the weak." You may be doing yourself and the other party a favor by asking for an apology. Often when those we've wounded voice their pain, remorse sets in, reflection ensues, and the result is a genuine "I'm sorry." You have no idea all the good that can come of confronting people about their offenses. They may get to thinking about others they have wounded. They may adopt a whole new attitude about acknowledging their wrongs and seeking forgiveness. You could be the catalyst for a turning point. So dare to help others. And if you do, don't approach them with words of rage. Loving-kindness and standing up for yourself are not mutually exclusive.

If you ask for an apology and you are rebuffed—yes, that's insult upon injury. You ought not despair, however. Don't think your effort was in vain, and please don't think yourself a sap. Your acknowledgment of the hurt and your willingness to speak up on the matter and start the peace process frees you up, lifts a load, and opens the way for healing to begin. You've done your job. You've given another person a chance to get righteous. Should he or she choose not to walk that road, you know for sure that you bear no blame or responsibility. Of course, in all likelihood your relationship with a person who refuses to apologize will change: once close may become distant, and once distant may become nonexistent. All you can do is look forward, guarding your heart against a demon more powerful than rum: revenge.

If you're hesitant about asking for an apology because you think doing this will make you a beggar, think again. Sometimes you have to "stoop to conquer." If you're skittish about asking for an apology because you can't believe that people really do this, then you haven't watched my show. Consider this sampling of issues men and women from all walks of life, of all temperaments, conditions, and hues, have had the courage to bring up on *Forgive or Forget*.

- *Patrick demanded an apology from Shannon for stealing the engagement ring that once was hers.*

These two young people had known each other for years and had been through quite a lot of drama (including Shannon once pretending to be pregnant and Patrick fooling around with one of Shannon's friends). It was probably a good thing that they broke off the engagement, and it was commendable that Patrick and Shannon tried to remain friends. But more drama ensued when, after Shannon moved out,

Patrick discovered that the engagement ring Shannon had returned to him was missing. Patrick was convinced that Shannon had stolen the ring, and he asked her to confess to the theft on the show. Shannon swore up and down that she was innocent, and Patrick swore that her failure to tell the truth meant the end of their friendship. The good news is, Shannon's conscience eventually kicked in. A few months later she returned to *Forgive or Forget* to come clean. She said that when she saw herself on television she felt so ashamed. She apologized to me—and more important, to Patrick, who came through the door, yes, but, boy oh boy, was he still fuming. Their friendship is a work-in-progress.

- *Nikki demanded an apology from her sister Pinky for not filing Nikki's taxes in 1996, as promised— and for not telling Nikki about her failure to do so until after April 15.*

Was Miss Pinky sorry? Was she ready to make restitution? Not at all. "Stop calling my house periodically," Pinky told her sister. "Do not send me no more messages . . . I am sick and tired of you—and, oh, well, if you didn't get your taxes done, that's your loss. I got mine and I enjoyed spending my money. Bye."

(Mother Love was thinking, One day Pinky's going to need Nikki for something.)

- *Piper asked her friend, Lisa, to apologize for not supporting her decision to get surgery for her obesity.*

Piper, who once weighed 450 pounds, weighed 195 pounds after gastric bypass surgery. Because Lisa believed this surgery was too dangerous, she had been loud and clear (and rather harsh) in her opposition to it. Two years had passed when Piper came on the show. Seeing the new Piper for the first time, Lisa gasped and shook her head in amazement. Lisa had never known exactly how much Piper weighed (Piper was quite tall and looks were deceiving), and so she never fully appreciated how much weight her friend was carrying around. Lisa admitted that she'd said some cruel things to Piper during their tiff about the surgery and she said that Piper was definitely due a *big* "I'm sorry."

- *Rob demanded an apology from his wife, Michelle, for getting their baby girl's ears pierced against his wishes.*

Rob was *so* mad. He went on and on about how his wife had no business traumatizing their daughter like that. Of course, the real issue wasn't the baby's ears getting pierced. The real issue was that wifey-pooh had defied Rob. This was about a power struggle. Was Rob's wife behind the door eager to apologize? No. Rob and Michelle's drama was among our earliest Empty Doors Revisited. The second time around, Rob was no less adamant and chauvinistic. ("I'm the boss!" he declared at one point.) When Rob, once again, faced an empty door, the audience applauded Michelle. And there was laughter—healthy laughter, because we all believed that Rob and Michelle (both very stubborn) truly loved each other and that it would take more than this clash over the baby's pierced ears to tear their marriage asunder.

• *Mossie demanded an apology from her former friend, Robin, for being a horrible friend.*

Mossie's list of injuries included the time Robin cheated Mossie out of the use of a rental car Mossie had paid for and Robin's calling her a "ho" and in other ways humiliating her in public. The high offense was Robin stranding Mossie at the annual frat party in Atlanta, Georgia, the Freaknic. This happened two years before Mossie aired her grievances on our show. Robin came through the door: she apologized for stranding Mossie in Atlanta, and even though she didn't remember humiliating Mossie in public, she apologized for that too. And then . . . Robin started bringing up stuff that Mossie owed her an apology for. These two young woman from my hometown, Cleveland, really began tripping at that point. There was a whole lot more to their story, I could tell, and I had serious doubts that Mossie and Robin would ever kick it again as friends.

- *Shelly demanded that her sister, Jenny, apologize for stealing her cell phone and running up a $225 bill.*

Jenny came through the door and gave her sister an apology for ripping her off and for at first lying about it. Along with the apology, Jenny gave her sister back her cell phone and said she wanted to make arrangements to pay off the debt. Though Shelley accepted Jenny's apology, I felt that the incident definitely broke a sister-love bond.

- *Hazel asked her sister Mercedes to apologize for stabbing her.*

Mercedes came through the door with an apology and tears that would not stop. "I am *so* sorry," were her first words. "I love you so much." Mercedes had been wracked with guilt for a long time—guilt over the knife wounds to her sister's face and body, guilt over the terrible rage she allowed herself to be consumed by the day they got into an altercation, guilt over all the trauma she'd put her family through, including her own daughter who was seven when she saw Mama pull a knife on Auntie. And Mercedes showed her sister no malice for testifying against her over the incident. (Mercedes had spent about a year and a half in jail.)

- *Valerie demanded an apology from her longtime friend, Pat, for not being there for her when her daughter died in a freak natural disaster.*

The background on this was in the news in September 1998, when a terrible storm hit the New York–New Jersey area. One of the casualties was Valerie's nineteen-year-old daughter, Edie, who was at a Labor Day outing when she was killed by a falling tree—right after she pushed her little brother out of harm's way. Pat was Edie's godmother and Valerie was godmother to Pat's son. Truly, these two women were as good as sisters. Their bond broke when Valerie, after hearing about her daughter's death, sent a message to Pat, asking her to baby-sit her son. Pat didn't show up, but only because she was caught up in her own trauma: her asthmatic son was in the hospital. Pat later called Valerie to apologize for not showing up, but Valerie, in her grief, wouldn't accept her apology, lashing out at Pat even to the point of blaming her for Edie's death. So Pat didn't go to Edie's wake or funeral. As she explained, she wasn't being spiteful; she had merely thought that staying away would be the best balm.

- *Darnell asked his younger sister to apologize for disrespecting him.*

Since the death of their parents Darnell had been taking care (and good care!) of his sister, but she didn't think she had to abide by any of his rules. And this rather unsweet sixteen-year-old did not apologize. (She even got flip with me—Wrong!) After a little more tough Mother Love, L'il Miss Sass apologized to her brother, and to me.

- *Erika demanded an apology from her former friend, Katrina, for making her look like a liar and getting her arrested.*

It all started when Erika told Katrina that her boyfriend was cheating on her. In a fit of anger over what she thought was spite work, Katrina tipped off the police about Erika's old arrest warrant for assault and battery, and Erika spent thirty days in jail. Did Katrina apologize? Yes, she did. (By the way, Katrina's boyfriend had indeed been cheating on her.)

- *Adelle and Charles demanded an apology from their daughter Linda for being disrespectful—and most of all for continuing to work as a stripper after she'd told them she had quit.*

Linda had really broken her parents' hearts. "It's putting a hole in our family," her mother said. Both parents expressed their love for Linda. Nevertheless, if Linda didn't change her ways (especially her job) she would no longer be welcomed in her parents' home. It was Charles, up in his seventies and a deacon in his church, who made the ultimatum point-blank clear. And the healing began when Linda, swearing off stripping, apologized to her parents on bended knee.

- *Bethany demanded that her son, Malachi, apologize for being a rebellious, troublesome, lazy-butt child.*

Bethany admitted that she had spoiled her son. Example: she set him up with an apartment, a car,

and an allowance of $500 a month when he was 18.
And every time wild-child Malachi got into a jam,
Bethany bailed him out. So Malachi lived a trifling,
hanging out life, refusing to get a real job and support himself, living on moms. Bethany had made
threats in the past, but now she was serious. Shape
up *and* ship out, she was saying. "I want a million wit-
nesses." This is why, she announced, she'd come on
Forgive or Forget. Her son came through the door,
hugged her, apologized (looking real smug), and said
he wanted to see her happy. He promised to move out
of his mother's place within two weeks. And as I
reminded Bethany, loving your children often means
being tough.

· *Jukima wanted her estranged husband, Micah, to*
  apologize for cheating on her (and that wasn't all).

Two days before he married Jukima, Micah had a
fling with a woman at his bachelor party, and the
woman ended up with child. A year passed before
Micah told Jukima about any of this and by then, their
marriage was shaky, with Micah giving Jukima reason
to think there were other-women problems (staying
away for days at a time will do it). After Micah told
Jukima about his prenuptial tryst, she tried to take her

life. The audience was hissing at Micah even before they met the man. When he walked through the door, the boos ballooned. He apologized, lamely, I thought (and I said as much). He didn't seem terribly grieved either when Jukima laid some sad news on him: during their separation she had lost the triplets she was carrying. Micah hadn't known she was pregnant. A woman in the audience said to Jukima, "Sweetheart, you don't need him," and to Micah, she said, "Hit the road, Jack!" When another woman asked Jukima if she wanted Micah back, Jukima said she preferred not to answer the question.

I have not shared these stories to start a stampede. I am not saying that you should hightail it to everyone who has wronged you with a request for an apology. Be selective. (For more on this, see passage 6.) But if you do decide to confront someone, consider doing it on *Forgive or Forget* (just call 1-877-APOLOGY). Mother Love won't let you fall.

Before you go asking for an apology, on *Forgive or Forget* or anywhere else, be sure your stuff is in order. It often happens that someone who is darn sure they are owed an apology is delusional.

Don't be petty like P. J., who came on the show to take her friend June to task for not keeping promises she made. According to P. J., when June received money from a huge lawsuit, she was going to splurge on P. J. and her family—toys and other treats for the kids and, for P. J., a tummy tuck and just about everything she'd need to launch a singing career. As it turned out, when June received the settlement (more than $1 million), P. J. and her children got next to zilch.

P. J. tried to convince us that she was more upset for her children than for herself, but it wasn't working (and the funky way she came out of her mouth didn't help). Also, June brought up some mitigating circumstances that made you go Hmmmm. Take for instance the fact that P. J. had cussed out June's husband. And then, there was the new car debacle: June had supplied the $2,000 down payment on a car for P. J., and when P. J. couldn't get financing for the balance due, June retrieved her money. Made sense to me; however, P. J. thought she should have been able to keep the $2,000. (And I will always believe that had P. J. played her cards right, June would have shared the wealth.)

And for goodness sake, don't be arrogant like Jennifer, a twenty-something-year-old who came on *Forgive or Forget* all ripped about her grandmother and aunt not being a part of her seven-month-old baby's life. She vehemently demanded an apology for the neglect. She almost took up a whole show! And the boo-hooing she did—even walked off the set when her aunt and grandmother told her they felt they had nothing to apologize for.

Were Auntie and Granny being cold? I didn't think so. Dig this: when Jennifer had her baby, her grandmother had just had triple-bypass surgery, and since the surgery Jennifer's aunt had been very busy taking care of the grandmother. Truth be told, when Grandma called Jennifer "a little snit!" and said, "It'll be a cold day in hell before I apologize," I said to myself, "You go, Granny!"

"Get a grip, Jennifer!" I told this young woman backstage. And on camera, I told her in no uncertain terms that she should have called her grandmother and her aunt, that she should have sent them photos of her new baby. I reminded her that she was the youngest of the adults and that all honor and respect are due to elders.

Jennifer left the show with an apology and with a four-generation reunion—Granny, Auntie, Recovering Snit, and Babycakes. That's what Jennifer needed. She also left with something equally important and useful for her future: a reality check.

This should serve as a reminder that no matter what the outcome of your request for an apology, it can be a win-win situation for you. If you receive an apology, you can enter into a healthier relationship with the person who wronged you. If you don't get the apology that you think is due, you may learn that your perspective was a bit out of kilter. Or you may learn that your vision was 20/20 and that you are a stronger, smarter, more loving person than you thought. You will also have learned not to give your power, joy, and strength to someone who's wronged you. I saw this play out in a powerful way in Francina's story.

When Francina was in the sixth grade her father molested her. Repeatedly. This eleven/twelve-year-old girl was afraid to tell her mother. She was afraid to tell anybody. But the truth came out. It came out when someone at her school called in counselors from social services. Francina had been acting out. As she herself admitted, she had started beating up little kids for no reason, sometimes for "just looking at me." On top of this, she'd cussed out a few of her teachers. "It was like I didn't care about the world," she said.

Francina ended up telling the counselors about what her father had been subjecting her to. Social services, in turn, alerted Francina's mother, Sharon. Back then, Francina probably couldn't have articulated what she wanted and expected from her mother now that she had been rescued and no longer had to keep her father's filthy secret.

As Francina recalled all these years later, when she came home from school after speaking with the counselors, her brothers met her in front of the house with a message from their mother: "She don't want to see your face and she don't want to talk to you. Don't come in her house." These are the words Francina remembered. "I thought my mother was going to be there for me," Francina cried, "but she wasn't. It's like she was mad at me for telling."

Francina went to her grandparents who lived next door.

When Sharon was informed about Francina's accusation against her father, she refused to believe that her husband could have done such a thing. She was convinced that Francina was telling a barefaced lie, and she kept thinking that until a doctor's report proved that there had been sexual abuse. Soon there was no way she could disbelieve Francina's charge, because her husband confessed. He was still in jail (he got twenty-seven years) when Francina came on *Forgive or Forget*.

Francina came on our show to demand an apology from her mother for at first not believing her and for turning her back on Francina after she knew the truth. Eight years had passed and Francina had not lived with her mother. There was no mother-daughter love going on. They were more like distant acquaintances. According to Francina, Sharon had never once talked with her about all that she had endured.

"I just hope that she'll take the time out to listen," Francina said, "and find out how I really felt when I was sitting there holding it all in and couldn't say nothing." Her tears were on the rise as she added, "I just want her to be my friend again."

When it was time for Francina to go over to the door and find out if her mother was willing to apologize and ready for them to finish healing together, I wanted to hold Francina's hand and make that short walk with her. But I couldn't. I had to follow the format. I had to abide by the principle that the guest takes "the walk" alone.

I helped Francina rise from the sofa with these words: "You know, this you have to do for yourself." As I rubbed her back and gave her my mother love, I said, "Come on, you're a tough girl. You've made it this far."

As Francina walked over to the door, my executive producer said in my ear, "Hang in there, Mother Love. You've got to stay focused. She needs your strength." I was on the verge of collapse, and praying, *Be there, be there. This child is broken. Her mother's love will help heal her, help mend her heart. This will be good. Oh, God, oh, God, what if Sharon's not there? Throw that out— this is her child, she'll be there. She has to be there.*

When the door opened to air and that black drape, Francina stood there for a beat as if frozen. Then, out of the depths of her soul, out of that place where deep calls to deep, there arose such a wailing, almost a howling. I forgot about format, television cameras, commercials. I rushed over to Francina, whose sobbing was growing louder, whose hands were pressed hard against her face as if she were trying to cover up nakedness, and whose knees had given way. By the time I reached her, she was almost on the floor, just about on her knees.

"I'm not going to let you fall," I said as I lifted Francina up. "I'm not going to let you fall apart." I could no longer keep back my own tears. "Hold on to me," I cried as I hugged her, as I rocked her. "Hold on to Mother Love." And she did, as if for dear life.

I later found out that at that moment there was hardly a dry eye in the house. Audience, staff, and crew alike were shocked, dismayed, even angry. Tears streamed down some faces. Many people just shook their heads. Other heads just hung, stunned.

I think that along with the consternation, the audience was feeling a great heartbreak, a deep heartache to witness a young soul so forsaken. There was an eerie silence in the studio.

I walked Francina back over to the sofa. When she sat down, she dropped her head, covered her eyes, and she cried and cried some more.

Then, the response of "Why?" All eyes, except for Francina's and mine, were on the big screen.

My instincts and the vibe from the audience said that it was best if I didn't look at Sharon when I asked in my best be-a-nice-host voice, "Sharon, what do you want to say to your daughter?"

"I want to tell her I don't owe her an apology."

My voice was not so nice when I asked, "That's all you have to say?"

"I had problems too," Sharon huffed back. "She's not the only one who had problems. I left her for a while, but I came back. I came back and I was right next door."

In another setting, I think a few folks in the audience would have jumped Sharon at this point. When she added, "She needs to grow up and go on with her life," it would have been mob rule.

Before I could snatch back a little of my be-a-nice-host voice, I blurted out to Sharon, "Wait a minute, can I just ask you—"

Before I could complete my sentence, Sharon snapped, "You can ask me anything you like."

I proceeded to ask Sharon if she'd been there emotionally for Francina. Sharon claimed that she had been, and she went on to say that Francina had always been a liar, which is why she hadn't believed her at first. She said Francina was lying about her brothers giving her the message that Sharon didn't want her to set foot in her house. Sharon said it was Francina's choice not to live with her. (OK. She say/She say, but I'm thinking that no child would choose not to live with her mother unless she was afraid of something.)

I let Sharon have her say and rationalize away what I thought was some very unmotherly behavior. As she saw it, she had had to get herself together so that she would be able to help Francina and her siblings.

"And this is what you call helping your daughter?" I was exclaiming by now. "No matter what kind of drama I'm going through, it's not going to be great enough for me to abandon my baby in her dark hour."

"You don't know what you're talking about," Sharon said.

Things between Sharon and me came close to getting a little street. We needed a break, but we could not break. The show had to go on. To change the air, I decided to let a few of my audience members have a chance at the mike.

Wouldn't you know it, the first person I went to was a woman as hot-tempered as I used to be. In her sound-off on Sharon she said, "You are no mother, no mother!"

Next, with great poise and compassion, a young woman urged Sharon to end the madness, to "get rid of your anger and move on."

Sharon was angry that she no longer had her husband, that he was in jail because Francina had opened her mouth. In her mind, Francina had destroyed their family.

"Yeah," Sharon snipped, "we both need to get rid of our anger and move on."

We were talking to a wall.

Nevertheless, I tried to reason with Sharon some more. "This child almost collapsed at that door," I said. "She almost fell out because her mother would not reach out to her." By now I was all choked up. I wanted to beg Sharon to come through the door. "I am a stranger to her. We're strangers to her. When this show is over she goes home with this pain." As I struggled not to burst into tears, I again forgot I was doing a show: I was one mother talking to another mother about loving her child. "And you mean to tell me," I continued, "that you can't find it in your heart to reach out to your own flesh and blood—no matter what is going on? If you're grieving, why can't you grieve together?"

The audience's applause reminded me where I was. And more than a few wanted a turn at the mike.

I made a point of going over to one of the more subdued-looking guests, a young man I thought would have something soothing or uplifting to say. Not.

"You are a disgrace to all mothers," this young man declared, "and a waste of a human being!"

That was low, but I couldn't get but so angry with this fellow, because I knew he meant well, that he spoke out of righteous indignation. Still, I had to put a check on the mean-spiritedness, the raw hostility that was directed at Sharon and that could easily have gotten out of hand—especially had I said that Sharon was still married to Francina's father and visited him regularly.

"No," I said to the young man, "I'm not going to let you say that, because if we lose hope we lose everything."

"She should come out, then."

"Yes, she should," I said, "Yes, she should! I don't disagree with you at all. I absolutely believe that she should have come through that door—"

I was spent. Whatever energy I had left I needed to focus on Francina, who still had her head down and her hands pressed over her face.

Back at Francina's side, I said, "I simply cannot imagine what you feel . . . but do you think just for a minute, just for a second, you can say something to her, tell her how you feel?" As I uttered these words I was praying that maybe, just maybe, if Sharon heard Francina talking directly to her, her heart might be softened and she might change her mind and come through the door.

Francina hesitated when I asked her to turn to the screen and talk to her mother. "You were scared before, you were by yourself before," I said, thinking about all those days she'd stuffed her pain, her rage. Then I reminded Francina that she was no longer alone and that she no longer had to be scared.

Tears rolled down Francina's face. Her lips trembled as finally she addressed her mother. "I might have did a lot of bad things in my day," she said, "but what my father did to me and you leaving me—that was the hurting-est feeling I could ever have in my life." As she began to sob, Francina added, "And if you don't ever talk to me again . . . I'll always love you even though you don't want to be my mother anymore."

With a sigh I said, "You know, that's really a powerful

statement coming from someone in so much pain, Sharon."

Sharon did not respond.

"You still want to be her mother?" I asked. "You know you're going to be, but do you want to be?"

"I still am," Sharon huffed.

"You are, but do you want to be?"

In a lick Sharon answered, "No, I don't *want* to be, but I still am."

The audience gasped, sighed, *ooh*ed, *aah*ed, and an angry rumble spread through the room.

I was *too* through. I was finished. I could not say another word to Sharon, because I knew that if I did I'd lose my talk show cool. I also knew that at that moment there was nothing I or anybody else could do to move Sharon to a better state of mind. And there was Francina with her head buried in my shoulder.

> The hammer that shatters the glass forges the steel.
>
> —Russian proverb

As the segment came to an end, I told Francina, "My hope and my strength and my faith tell me to tell you,

'You be strong.' This didn't kill you. It'll make you stronger. It'll make you tougher." Francina's head was still bowed, but she was sitting up now. As I nudged her chin up, I reaffirmed that what her father had put her through had been atrocious. "But you hold your head up and you be proud," I said, "because you have survived this. You are by no means junk, a chump, or a wuss." I also reminded Francina that she had done a great and mighty thing in coming on *Forgive or Forget*, in wanting things to be right between her and her mother. "So you don't let this take you," I said. "You are a lot tougher than you think."

When the cameras stopped rolling, the audience was dismissed and Francina was on her way back to her life. She was stronger, smarter, freer, and more forgiving than even I thought she could, should, or would be.

I do not believe that sheer suffering teaches. If suffering alone taught, all the world would be wise, since everyone suffers. To suffering must be added mourning, understanding, patience, love, openness, and the willingness to remain vulnerable.

— Anne Morrow Lindbergh

Francina's story was one of the hardest segments I had ever done. It is also one of the most precious because it was so affirming. I will carry it with me forever. It took me to another level of insight on the power of forgiveness and the possibilities of overcoming. It reminded me that we never know what wounds people are walking around with and so it behooves us all to be as kind as possible, especially to strangers. As often happens, the audience's response to Francina's pain was evidence that despite the raging cynicism and skepticism in our land, there are still lots of people who believe in such things as right and wrong. There are lots of people who are not strangers to compassion.

These observations came later. When the segment was over, I couldn't put two thoughts together. I was a mess. I was spent, drained, lost. I cried for what seemed like hours. Francina's story was the first of three stories we would tape for that show. (We tape two shows a day, with three or four segments per show.) I had known it was going to be one of the tougher ones, which is why I had suggested that we make it the last. Instead, it ended up being the first one, and so much tougher than I had imagined. It had taken more out of me than I knew I had. And next on deck was Dana apologizing to his brother,

Jerry, for getting him jailed, stealing his girlfriend, and causing him to lose millions of dollars in business, his house, car, and just about everything he owned. Nobody told me there'd be days like this.

I didn't think I could handle another tragedy between family members. I had a tough time looking forward and preparing emotionally for the rest of the segments because my mind stayed on Francina. Had I said the right things? Had my heart been in the right place?

The show's resident therapist assured me that I had done all right with Francina, that I had not done anything that she had to undo when she spoke with Francina.

The response to Francina's story was beyond overwhelming. The show aired on a Wednesday in March 1999, and by the end of the day we had received roughly two hundred calls about that segment alone. The next day there were more calls about Francina's story, and by Friday the total had climbed to six hundred.

People had called to vent their anger at Sharon. People had called to urge us to do whatever we could to get Sharon to come around. Most of the calls were pure expressions of love for Francina: people wanted us to know that they were going to pray for her, that they had been inspired and encouraged by her courage and her hope, inspired and encouraged to forgive somebody or a whole lot of somebodies, or to apologize for a long-ago offense, or to count their blessings.

A few of the callers were people who had molested a child and were deeply, deeply sorry. Several callers said that they too had been molested by a relative and then kicked to the curb by their mothers. One woman said she wished she had someone to hold her as I had held Francina.

A most memorable message came from a Californian named Barbara. In her voice mail, she said, in part:

> *I watched the show that aired on March 3, the segment on that young girl who was molested by her father. Mother Love was absolutely wonderful and she can't even imagine how many people she healed today when she held that child in her arms. I am a victim of the same type of circumstances, not with my father but with my brother. It was very healing what she did for me. I would like to thank you for putting on that show. Mother Love was flawless and perfect.*

STEP #6

You Don't Have to Receive an Apology to Forgive

Some people do not have the guts to say "I'm sorry"—not even after you have expressed to them your hurt and asked for an apology. Some people may indeed want to offer you an apology, but they don't know how to find you. Some people who have wronged you may be dead.

In such cases, can you forgive? I hope you will try.

One of the secrets of a long and fruitful life is to forgive everybody everything every night before you go to bed.

—Ann Landers

An apology is definitely a balm; however, when it comes to a deep release the key isn't the apology really; it's your decision to forgive. So forgiving should always be our first focus, not receiving an apology.

I am a witness that you can forgive when there's no apology: I've done it several times.

A so-called manager during the early part of my career as a stand-up comic never apologized for skipping out on me with money I had earned, yet I forgave him (and years later he wanted to take big-time credit for my career—that man had no shame).

I forgave the so-called friend who, eons ago, convinced me that California would be my land of milk and honey, but after I trekked out there she turned out to be a flat-leaver. I ended up stranded in the City of Angels with no home, no honey, no gigs, and with a two-year-old strapped to my hip.

I have also had opportunities to forgive people I did not know, like the people who robbed my house one Christmastime.

It was 1977. I was working as a playground leader for the Parks Department in Columbus, Ohio. My husband was working too and making OK money but nothing grand. So we were surviving. Extras required scrimping and saving, not to mention careful planning. A big and bountiful Christmas was one

of the extras to which I had always been committed.
At the top of every year, I started my Christmas fund
and contributed to it faithfully. I always put my deco-
rations up on December 1. Among my friends and
family, I was most always the first to get Christmas
cards out. "Girl," my friends would say, "you just
always gotta put everybody in the Christmas spirit!"
Yes, I did, and I always put plenty of forethought into
gifts.

The Christmas of 1977 was a Christmas I had
planned on making extra special, extra spirited, because it was my son Jahmal's first Christmas. Come
Christmastime, he would be seven months old. I'd been
daydreaming on his first Christmas since I was pregnant with him.

As usual, for the Christmas of 1977 I did most of
my gift-buying in one fell swoop (remember: I start
thinking about gifts in January). On this mid-
November day, as usual, when I headed home from
the store, I was wonderfully heavy-laden. My car was
crammed. The trunk was full. The backseat was full.
You couldn't see the floor of the car. The passenger
seat was piled high, and only the driver's side window
and half of the windshield weren't blocked. Fortun-
ately, I made it home without a fender bender or a
cop spotting me. It took me maybe five or six hefty

trips to get everything into my apartment. Phew! But it was so worth it.

It was a workday, so after I unloaded everything I beat it to the park. When I came home for lunch, I delighted over my big shop, and as I left for work again I fancied how much fun I was going to have wrapping presents when I got back.

When I returned home, my living room was naked. Every one of the gazillion presents—gone! Not only that, but the thieves had snatched some of my food from the refrigerator, including eight bottles of my baby's milk (*my breast milk*). Several giant boxes of diapers (I have always been a bulk shopper) were also gone. They took my tea kettle. They took my iron, which had been atop my ironing board, which stood in front of the kitchen window through which they entered and left (leaving my ironing board all crippled up on the floor).

I was in no mood to be gracious.

Even before I called the police I had a feeling some of my neighbors were responsible for the robbery, but I never accused any one of them. I didn't know how much longer we'd be living there, but I knew we would-n't be moving out anytime soon. So self said to self, "Girl, y'all gotta live here for a while, so you can't be bulling up and hating these people and plotting revenge." I let it go. I stopped studying it and just went on being peaceable to my neighbors—the ones I strongly suspected had masterminded the robbery along with those I suspected knew for certain who the thieves were. "Forgive, forgive," that was my mantra. "Let go and let God," I kept telling myself.

I had to get in the mood to be gracious. And don't think it wasn't hard, especially when my stuff walked up on me.

In the days following the break-in, I saw more than a few people on the block enjoying what I was sure was my bounty. (And you know how you *know* your stuff!) There was the day I noticed that the teen mother who lived next door had her infant in the cutest outfit. Hmmmm, I thought, that looks just like the outfit I bought for my baby. Another day, I swear I saw another neighbor's four-year-old toddling around with a bottle of my breast milk. (And you know how you *know* your stuff!)

One of the most lasting pleasures you can experience is the feeling that comes over you when you genuinely forgive an enemy—whether he knows it or not.

—O. A. Battista

Self had to keep talking to self: "Girl, remember you still have to live here, and you don't want these people targeting you again." The rage went away, and I went on looking forward to my son's first Christmas.

My husband contributed his last two paychecks to my now empty Christmas fund. He told me to spend it any way I wanted to. I didn't. I used it sparingly, focused on replacing some of the things I had purchased for our son.

Christmas Day was blessed. Friends and family came over as planned. The food was plentiful and good. My son was healthy and happy. It was very sentimental, and one of my best Christmases. With the reduction of presents, I was really able to see that the Christmas spirit wasn't about stuff. I'd always known that intellectually, but for the first time I was knowing it experientially—I was living it. I think the cheer that overflowed from our house shocked certain of the neighbors. Certain ones continued to avoid my eyes whenever our paths crossed during the next year and a half that my family lived in that apartment.

The art of being wise is the art of knowing what to overlook.

—William James

You can work your way up to forgiving big offenses for which you don't expect an apology by practicing on the everyday things that pinch and tick you off. Think about it. Don't you find yourself nursing minigrudges over what is really stupid stuff—a mud-splashed coat, a taken cab, a taken parking space, others being late for a meeting, horrific traffic, your loud kids, your quiet man, your mother calling for the fifth time (be glad you can hear her voice), your roommate leaving a swallow of juice in the carton, your friend not being kind when it comes to rewinding the videos she borrows. Pick one!

A clever person turns great troubles into little ones and little ones into none at all.

—Chinese proverb

Every day offers a round of opportunities for forgiveness, to help you get to . . . tomorrow.

STEP #7

Forgiving Is Not Forgetting

> The stupid neither forgive nor forget, the naïve forgive and forget, the wise forgive but do not forget.
>
> —Thomas Szasz

If you think forgiving an injury means tossing it out of your mind, think again. I don't believe this is logical. What's more, I don't think most of us can do this. The issue is not "How do I forgive and forget?" but "What am I to do with the memory?"

To answer that question, I need to start with what not to do with the memory: namely, don't dwell on it. Don't replay the wrong over and over in your mind.

Don't tell anybody and everybody about it—especially the busybody types who relish stirring up dirt and making mud. The more you think about something, the more you talk about it, the more power it gains, the bigger it becomes. There's nothing to be gained from rehashing bad news.

While you should not dwell, obsess, and build a shrine to an injury, you should definitely hold onto the lesson in the experience. And most every terrible thing that happens to us has a lesson, sometimes two or three.

Let's say a friend who has a history of being a big-mouth betrayed a confidence: you should remember this because, while bearing the blabber no malice, you need to never again tell her a secret.

Let's say someone borrowed something from you and never returned it (and may even have copped an attitude when you asked about it): you'd be wise to think twice about letting that person borrow any-thing you care about again. The same applies if the next time you saw the item it was damaged. This hap-pened to me when I let one of my girlfriends in col-lege borrow one of my superbad tops.

It was a really cute black top. It sported an appliqué of a woman's face with a hat cocked over one eye—very stylish at the time, the kind of thing a retro freak might pay high dollars for today. I had three of these bad mamajammers: one black, one red, and one some other color that escapes me. So when my friend asked to borrow my brand-new never-put-my-body-print-in-it lady top, I could afford to be a little generous. I rarely let people borrow my clothes, but I thought she was cool. I had never been over to her house, but I knew she had a baby, so I figured she was mature and clean and—I was so wrong!

I first figured something was up when she didn't return my lady top in a timely fashion. I didn't get too bent out of shape, though, because I figured she'd do the right thing soon.

Soon wasn't soon.

One day she invited me over to her pad. OK, I was thinking, this will be the right time and the right place to bring up my lady top—but then I probably won't have to, because she's a stand-up chick.

Hers wasn't the kind of pad I'd want to spend the night in—or eat in for that matter. And when I got a chance to check out her bedroom, what was the first thing I saw? My superbad lady top balled up on the floor—dirty, filthy.

"What in the—"

This chick was like, "Girl, I'ma clean it up."

Yeah, right, I thought as I picked up my lady top. Not only was it *funky*, but half of the lady face was unappliquéed. This was back in the 1970s, and I had paid $35 or $40 for that shirt!

"That's all right," I said. "I don't even want it back."

This incident put a damper on our friendship. I decided I would be doing us both a favor if I never allowed her to borrow anything else from me again. ("Fool me once, shame on you; fool me twice . . ."— you know the drill.)

Another thing I've learned not to forget is who among my family I should never lend money to, because they never repay. If I have it to give, I give, but letting deadbeats borrow—

"Can you just loan me—"

"No, not happening. I ain't loaning you eye-water to cry with. No."

I think one should forgive and remember. . . . If you forgive and forget in the usual sense, you're just driving what you remember into the subconscious; it stays there and festers. But to look, even regularly, upon what you remember and *know* you've forgiven is an achievement.

—Faith Baldwin

Some think me Scrooge, and I'm comfortable with that. I forgive them, but I don't forget that they do not keep their word. And if I lend them money, I'm only encouraging them in a character flaw.

And remember that Christmas robbery I told you about a few pages back? Yes, I forgave the people who robbed me, but I didn't forget that they had entered through my kitchen window. Though I didn't want to borrow trouble, I figured I'd better take some precautions. So I reached back into my grandmother's bag of antitheft devices. I got a strong piece of vinyl onto which I glued rocks and bits of glass and other sharp stuff. Every night before we went to sleep and whenever we left the apartment, I laid that bad boy out in front of my kitchen window.

So, no, forgiving doesn't mean forgetting. If you forget, you're liable to keep taking crap off people or cosigning their nonsense. It's a false paradox to think that you can't forgive and at the same time protect yourself.

STEP #8

If It's Over, Let It Be Over

Let the past drift away with the water.

—Japanese saying

When you forgive, take it to the max. Don't take one step forward and two steps back.

Don't talk about the matter with others unless they really need to know. And for goodness sake don't hold the offense over the person's head. That's what a couple who came on *Forgive or Forget* did, and it almost wrecked their marriage. These two really did love each other, but somehow they'd let what should have been bygones be bullies.

Before they were married, the two, whom I like to call Jack and Jill, had both played love buddy with other people when their relationship was supposed to be exclusive. Their infidelities weren't more powerful than their love. Jack and Jill forgave each other, started a renewed romance, and eventually heard wedding bells.

Never pour water over a drowned mouse.

—Irish proverb

Weirdly, after they were married, every time they got into an argument, instead of staying on track with the issue, they would backtrack. They had lied to each other (and to themselves) about forgiving, and their drama would go something like this:

Jack would snipe, "Well, you cheated on me!"

So Jill would snap, "Don't forget that you had cheated on me!"

Then Jack would ratchet it up with, "I caught you in the bed with your ex-boyfriend!"

And Jill would come back with, "It never would have happened if you hadn't been cheating on me!"

Back and forth, back and forth—absurdity, with their children listening to them throw old dirt up in each other's face.

One day, Jill came into some sense. When, in the midst of a spat, Jack brought up her infidelity, she didn't play along. Nevertheless, he would persist in castigating her for her long-ago sin.

Forgiveness ought to be like a canceled note, torn in two and burned up, so that it can never be shown against the man.

—Henry Ward Beecher

Enough is enough! One day Jill reached the breaking point. She came on *Forgive or Forget* to demand that Jack apologize for the rewind. She also gave him an ultimatum: either really forgive me or I'm going to forget this marriage.

Jack was one of those manly-man men, so it was something when, with the world watching him up on that big screen, his eyes welled up and the floodgates opened.

Life can only be understood backwards; but it must
be lived forwards.

—Sören Kierkegaard

When he came through the door, he said, "I love
my wife so much. And I'm just not going to do this
any more." Now he had truly forgiven, and Jill forgave
him for the cheating and for throwing her infidelity
in her face. You could see them turn a corner in their
relationship. It was awesome.

"I feel sorry for them. . . . I don't hate the perpetrators. . . . In order to hate someone it would take a lot away from your own life. And I have a life to live. . . . I want to go on and be a sparkle in my dad's eye."

These words were spoken on Forgive or Forget by Renée Mullen, daughter of James Byrd, Jr. She and her younger sister, Jamie Byrd, appeared on our show shortly after their devastation.

It was in the early morning hours of June 7, 1998, that James Byrd, Jr., while walking home from a friend's anniversary party, accepted a lift from three men in a pickup truck. Instead of being taken home, Byrd was taken to a remote area where he was savagely beaten. Then the men, one of whom Byrd knew, chained him to the back of the pickup truck by his ankles and dragged him several miles down an empty Jasper, Texas, road. Byrd's body was torn asunder.

James Byrd was black, the men arrested for his murder—Lawrence Brewer, Shawn Berry, and John King—were white, and there's never been a scintilla of doubt that this was a race-hate crime.

Who among us would have been surprised if Byrd's daughters had nothing but venomous words for Brewer, Berry, and King? But no, Renée and Jamie, while deeming the death penalty just punishment for the deed, did not harbor hatred.

*These two poised, tender young women had come on
Forgive or Forget not to vent anger, but to let people
know what a good man their father had been, to express
their gratitude for the prayers and support of untold
people, and to urge people across the nation to do all in
their power to prevent such a thing as happened to their
father from happening to another soul. Renée and Jamie
hoped for healing and racial harmony.*

*While I sat with Renée and Jamie, I read a letter that
John King's father had released to the media.*

My sympathy goes out to the Byrd family.
There is no reason for a person to take the life
of another. And to take it in such a manner is
beyond any kind of reasoning. It hurts me
deeply to know that a boy I raised . . . could
find it in himself to take a life. This deed
cannot be undone, but I hope that we can all
find it in our hearts to go forward in peace and
with love for all. Let us find in our hearts love
for our fellow man. Hate can only destroy.
Again, I say to you, I'm sorry.

*Small tears rolled down the faces of Renée and Jamie at
several points during the segment, and the compassion
flowing from the audience to them was mighty.*

As my time with Renée and Jamie drew to an end, I asked if they thought they could forgive the men who killed the man they characterized as a "people person," the man they remembered as a concerned and caring father.

They admitted that they had not truly forgiven Brewer, Berry, and King; however, the wonder thing, the marvel of their souls, is that they truly wanted to forgive, and they were already on that journey. Said Renée, "I know I'll have to forgive them in order for me to make it into heaven."

Now What?

On the following pages, I offer you space to start your forgiveness journey: a place to list the things for which you need to forgive yourself, the people you owe an apology, and the people you need to forgive.

As you make these lists, don't clutter yourself with issues of priority, urgency, major, and minor. Just let it flow: fill in the blanks as things come to your remembrance.

After you've made your lists (or at least made a valiant start), consider treating yourself to one of those nice blank books for recording how and when you deal with each issue and the outcomes of your efforts.

I need to forgive myself for . . .

1. _____

2. _____

3. _____

4. _____

5. _____

6. _____

7. _____

8. _____

9. _____

10. _____

And if you can think of others, keep on.

I need to apologize to . . .

1. _____ *for* _____

2. _____ *for* _____

3. _____ *for* _____

4. _____ *for* _____

5. _____ *for* _____

6. _____ *for* _____

7. _____ *for* _____

8. _____ *for* _____

9. _____ *for* _____

10. _____ *for* _____

You're on a roll!

I need to forgive . . .

1. _____ *for* _____

2. _____ *for* _____

3. _____ *for* _____

4. _____ *for* _____

5. _____ *for* _____

6. _____ *for* _____

7. _____ *for* _____

8. _____ *for* _____

9. _____ *for* _____

10. _____ *for* _____

Look how well you're mending. You can do this!

And here's a little something else for you to ponder.

F   is for *Finally realizing it should be done.*

O   is for *Opening your heart.*

R   is for *Really meaning to let go.*

G   is for *God's light in you.*

I   is for *Individual responsibility.*

V   is for *Very gently loving one another.*

E   is for *Every heart deserves forgiveness.*

N   is for *Never underestimating the power in you.*

E   is for *Everlasting peace.*

S   is for *Sanity of your spirit.*

S   is for *Sharing your love.*

Now come up with your own acrostic. Should you care to share it with me, send it to *Forgive or Forget*, 460 West 42nd Street, New York, New York, 10036 or E-mail me at www.forgiveorforget.com.

F   is for   _____

O   is for   _____

R   is for   _____

G   is for   _____

I   is for   _____

V   is for   _____

E   is for   _____

N   is for   _____

E   is for   _____

S   is for   _____

S   is for   _____

You've read the book.
You've started the journey.
You're learning the passages.
Now, continue on.

I am Mother Love, and remember—

Never underestimate the power of forgiveness!